Silver Link Silk Editions
SLP

Lament for a Branch Line
The Preston to Southport Railway

Foreword by Sir Peter Hendy CBE

© David Hindle 2021

All rights reserved. No part of this publication may be reproduced, stored in a retrieval system or transmitted, in any form or by any means, electronic, mechanical, photocopying, recording or otherwise, without prior permission in writing from Silver Link Books, Mortons Media Group Ltd.

First published in 2021
Enlarged 2nd Edition published in 2022

British Library Cataloguing in Publication Data
A catalogue record for this book is available from the British Library.

ISBN 978 1 85794 609 3

Silver Link Books
Mortons Media Group Limited
Media Centre
Morton Way
Horncastle
LN9 6JR
Tel/Fax: 01507 529535

email: sohara@mortons.co.uk
Website: www.nostalgiacollection.com

Printed and bound in the Czech Republic

The British invented the railway, and its development into a national network changed the country economically and socially into an industrialised nation in much less than 100 years. Our great main lines are almost entirely still with us, but the many secondary and branch lines, which did as much for their local areas as the main lines did for big cities and cross-country travel, in many cases, sadly, are not.

This very comprehensive book about the Preston to Southport railway tells an extraordinary story of one such lost railway. It has all the classic ingredients: the hopes of the promoters, the struggle to raise money, locomotives bought by a rich railway director for the line in the absence of enough money to buy its own, bankruptcy, takeover, the high point of Edwardian holiday traffic, then decline and closure. In addition, there are also a couple of branch lines, and the purchase and operation of a pleasure steamer (but not successfully, and not for long)!

In their time these railways changed their localities, enabling locals and visitors to travel to work and for leisure, and goods to be sent and received. Before the days of mass car ownership the railway became a vital institution, and many of the fascinating pictures in this volume record as much social as railway history.

The images of decline, the last trains and closure are melancholy but, in hindsight, inevitable. The world changed, and personal mobility with cars and goods by lorry left these lines anachronisms in the modern age.

But with the expert guidance of an author, who has comprehensively researched his subject, we can follow the story from inception to the present day, not only with objective clarity, but with affection and nostalgia for the past. This is an excellent history and record of one of Britain's secondary railways; I hope you enjoy it as much as I have.

Sir Peter Hendy CBE
Chair
Network Rail
Waterloo Station, London SE1

July 2021

Frontispiece: BR 'Standard' 'Clan' 4-6-2 No 72007 *Clan Macintosh* heads the RCTS Ribble Lune railtour near New Longton on 23 May 1964. *Peter Fitton*

Lament for a Branch Line

The Preston to Southport Railway

David John Hindle MA

A Silver Link Book

Contents

Introduction — 5
A tribute to Roger Ronald Roberts (1964-2020) — 10
Background to Preston and Southport during the Victorian era — 12

Chapter One	The Victorian 'railway mania' and its aftermath	19
Chapter Two	The origin and construction of the West Lancashire Railway	32
Chapter Three	The Liverpool, Southport & Preston Junction Railway	47
Chapter Four	The Tarleton branch and PS *Virginia*	58
Chapter Five	Operations on the West Lancashire Railway	64
Chapter Six	Aspirations, subsumption, Grouping and nationalisation	72
Chapter Seven	'All stations to Southport'	95
Chapter Eight	The heyday of the Preston to Southport branch	121
Chapter Nine	Modernisation: the beginning of the end	131
Chapter Ten	A night to remember: 6 September 1964	135
Chapter Eleven	Not au revoir but goodbye to the Preston to Southport branch	142
Chapter Twelve	Memories: lament for a branch line	151
Appendix One	Serious railway accident at Whitehouse Triangle, 13 May 1950: extract from the official report	172
Appendix Two	The ex-L&YR Aspinall Class 2P 'Radial' 2-4-2Ts at Southport	172

Bibliography — 174
Acknowledgements — 175

Index of locations — 176

The author's royalties from the sale of this book will be proportionally donated to charitable institutions including Grimsargh St Michael's Church fabric fund.

Introduction

It was to be the golden age of railways that fed Lancashire's seaside resorts. Blackpool and Southport had more miles of railway and stations than many other towns of a comparable size. The West Lancashire Railway (Preston to Southport direct) began life quite late when viewed against the boom years of railway construction, which had started in the mid-1830s at the time of the 'railway mania'. The 14¾-mile line was opened on 5 September 1882, in time for the Preston Guild celebrations of that year. For centuries 'Preston Guild' has been associated with civic, commercial and cultural events in the town (which is now a city).

By the time of the mid-20th century the Preston to Southport branch symbolised the rural branch line of the pre-Beeching era, and even today I still think about its characteristic regular locomotives, stations and structures, several of which had their origins with the Lancashire & Yorkshire Railway (L&YR). Inextricably woven into a pattern of rural life, it was the quintessence of a northern branch line in a landscape bedecked with greenhouses and agricultural holdings in endless fertile fields. With double track throughout its length, there was much pleasure in travelling in a forgotten railway age that had existed since the late Victorian era.

A distinctive feature of the branch was the swing bridge crossing the River Douglas at Hesketh Bank. Stanier 2-6-4T No 42435, with the 1.50pm Preston to Southport service, crosses the bridge on 8 August 1964. *David Hampson*

Stanier No 42662 heads a Southport to Preston service in pastoral countryside at Penwortham on 2 March 1963. *David Hampson*

Rural bliss in the halcyon days of the branch line, with Class 5 No 44686 hauling the 4.14pm Southport to Preston service towards the distinctive arched occupation bridge at Penwortham, Cop Lane station. *Chris Spring*

The epitome of a branch line: for many years the branch was worked by Stanier 3MT 2-6-2Ts from Southport shed, and one such engine, No 40197, is illustrated at the rural station of Banks. *John Williams*

Stanier 2-6-4T No 42565, Southport-bound, approaches New Longton & Hutton in the spring of 1963. *Stanley Withers*

Fairburn No 42132 enters Banks station bunker-first with a return Southport to Preston service on 2 September 1964. *The late Frank Dean, Malcolm Richardson collection*

Most of the stations were still fully staffed with station masters, ticket office staff, porters, signalmen and crossing keepers, collectively providing employment for about 200 people. Accordingly operating costs were high, and in terms of the income generated the maths did not add up!

As late as 1964 people living in Hundred End, Hesketh Bank, Hoole and other rural and suburban areas of south-west Lancashire could catch a train into Southport or Preston for main-line connections, but then along came Dr Richard Beeching, complete with a terminal syringe! On 6 September 1964, ironically almost 82 years to the day since the first passenger service had triumphantly run the full length of the new West Lancashire Railway, the service was no more, and the branch became a victim of the Beeching cuts.

The evocative role of a rural branch line is personified at the country station of Banks, with its signal box and passengers alighting from three non-corridor carriages on 2 September 1964. *The late Frank Dean, Malcolm Richardson collection*

A special niche is reserved in railway history for those great days of steam trains and rolling stock and the branch lines they served. With hindsight I was too young to realise the gravity of the closure, though I am reminded that the charm of this branch line was that it resembled a large-scale working museum, but alas with no further admittance. For me it evokes personal memories of travelling by train to Southport during the early 1960s, and it remains a

Above: Ivatt Class 5 No 44686 is pictured near Banks leaving the urban conurbations behind and heading for open country with the 11.18am Southport to Preston service *Arnold Battson*

Above right: As a boy I stood in awe of steam locomotives seen from the footbridge alongside the ELR viaduct, typified by Fairburn No 42154 powering a train from Preston to Colne in the spring of 1962. *Stanley Withers*

Right: A wintry scene on the East Lancashire line overlooking Avenham Park in February 1958. *Arnold Battson*

Above: Hundred End signal box in the mid-20th century was delightfully old-fashioned, but it worked. *Roger Roberts*

Above right: Aspinall No 52456 characterises branch-line workings in the mid-20th century as it descends from Churchtown with the 5.56pm Preston to Southport service on 23 May 1956. *Ribble Steam Railway*

Right: Old-fashioned ex-L&YR Aspinall Class 2P 'Radial' 2-4-2T No 50746 is seen on station pilot duties at Southport Chapel Street. *Roger Roberts*

Introduction

personal sadness that the not so permanent way passed into history. In September 1984, on the 20th anniversary of the closure of the line, I began collecting material for a book on the branch and its chequered history interspersed with anecdotal material. I now wish to share the fruits of my labour and tell the story of a branch line that once ran across the West Lancashire plain from Preston to Southport.

Right: A Preston to Southport train, hauled by Riddles BR 'Standard' Class 2MT 2-6-0 No 78041, on the last day of service Sunday 6 September 1964. The very last train from Preston to Southport departed at 10.30pm that night hauled by Fairburn 2-6-4T No 42061. *Rob Greenwood*

Below left: No 78041 carries the 'Last Day' headboard at Preston. The original Butler Street entrance to the ELR is shown on the left. *Rob Greenwood*

Below: Thereafter the branch, its quaint steam engines and stations, including Cop Lane, were just a memory. *Alan Castle*

Below right: A lasting souvenir, and time for a pint. *Alan Castle*

A tribute to Roger Ronald Roberts (1964-2020)

I dedicate this work to the memory of my work colleague and good friend, Roger Ronald Roberts. Roger amassed a unique photographic portfolio of the Preston to Southport line, which he bequeathed to me to share with all railway historians and enthusiasts and as a testament to the golden age of steam railways. Rodge died on 5 January 2020, and at his funeral service a poem, adapted by his family from Henry Van Dyke's 'Gone From My Sight', was read by his daughter, drawing an analogy of Roger's precious memory with his love of railways:

'I am standing upon a platform. A steam train at my side fuels the engine in the morning breeze and starts gracefully down the line. He is an object of beauty and strength. I stand and watch him until at length his smoke hangs like a speck of white cloud where the land and sky come to mingle with each other.
Then someone at my side says, "There he has gone."
Gone where?
Gone from my sight, that is all. He is just as large as boiler, cylinder and piston as he was when he left my side, and he is just as able to bear his living freight to his destined station.
His diminished size is in me – not in him.
And just at the moment when someone at my side says, "There he is gone," there are other eyes watching him coming, and there are voices waiting to take up the glad shout, "Here he comes!"'

Fairburn No 42061 waits at Preston with a Southport train on 6 September 1964. The next day the branch was consigned to railway history. To quote Henry Van Dyke's poem: 'There, he is gone.' *Ribble Steam Railway*

A tribute to Ronald Roger Roberts (1964-2020)

Above: BR 'Standard' Class 2-6-0 No 78041 carries the 'Last Day' headboard at Churchtown station on the same day. *Charles Box, Cedric Greenwood collection*

Above right: Ex-works Stanier No 42647 arrives at Preston East Lancs with a Southport to Preston service on 28 July 1964. *Peter Fitton*

Right: Fairburn 2-6-4 No 42296 and Stanier 2-6-4 No 42435 'take five' at Preston East Lancs Carriage Sidings on 7 April 1964. *Chris Spring*

Background to Preston and Southport during the Victorian era

In the mid to late Victorian era the two Lancashire towns of Preston and Southport could not have been more opposite in character and demographic profile. In 1871 Southport had a population of only 18,086, rising to 32,206 ten years later. There was very little industry outside the main sources of livelihood, which were fishing and farming. Preston's population rose from 85,427 in 1871 to 96,524 in 1881. The town was heavily reliant on the textile industry, engineering and the trade passing through the port.

Preston is especially famous for its Guild Merchant conferred by ancient charter, drawn up by the town's burgesses in 1179, to implement the trading and mercantile sections of the charters. Although the Guild had its origins during the reign of Henry II, the first documented Guild meeting is in 1397, during the reign of King Richard II, though it was only after 1542, during the reign of Henry VIII, that the 20-year cycle was adopted. The sequence of Preston Guilds every 20 years has only been interrupted once in 1942, when the Guild was cancelled because of wartime hostilities. Guild Year 1882 coincided with the opening of the West Lancashire Railway (WLR) and Preston's new Fishergate Hill station, which opened prematurely to accommodate special trains.

In Preston there were few bridges spanning the River Ribble. Penwortham Old Bridge was constructed in 1759 to link Broadgate with Penwortham, but exclusively for the use of pedestrians, carts and carriages. Alongside Penwortham Old Bridge, the WLR bridge was built in 1882 to link Preston with Southport. Nearby the land for the embryonic Avenham and Miller parks at Preston was donated by Thomas Miller, a local cotton manufacturer. The parks were created by unemployed textile workers at the time of the infamous cotton famine of the early 1860s. A 'harmonious whole' was the aim of the landscape architect, Edward Milner, when designing and creating these two Victorian masterpieces. With the two parks being divided by the ornate railway arches of the historic East Lancashire Railway (ELR) viaduct (1850), this ambience was definitely captured.

With the opening of the Park Hotel and the West Lancashire Railway, the *Preston Guardian* of 2 September 1882 reported that Preston's brand-new Gaiety Palace Theatre of Varieties music hall featured a backdrop embellished with the new luxury Park Hotel. In Preston and the growing coastal resort of Southport electric tramcars were gradually replacing earlier modes of public transport, and traction engines were replacing horses for the haulage of heavy industrial materials and for

Preston's 1759 Broadgate bridge. *R. C. Chown, Roger Roberts collection*

Background to Preston and Southport during the Victorian era

Left: An aerial view of Preston showing the town's station the ELR goods sidings and viaduct, and the Park Hotel overlooking the Miller and Avenham parks. *Copyright Aero Films (ref 13871)*

Right: The Park Hotel, Preston.

Below: The old Victorian Town Hall, Fishergate, Preston.

Below left: A police sergeant escorts a Preston tram. *Roger Roberts collection*

A period postcard of The Promenade, Southport.

Steam in the landscape of the rich arable land of the south-western plains of Lancashire, with Stanier 2-6-4T No 42662 at Much Hoole and a Stanier Class 5 near Banks on 24 August 1964. *Both David Hampson*

agricultural use. The automobile had yet to arrive and revolutionise road transport, which was to compete with the railway network.

Between the two towns of Preston and Southport lay a flat area of rich dark soil, part reclaimed from the sea and in some areas drained from peat bogs to provide fertile agricultural land, which ran through this sparsely populated district and followed the course of the south bank of the River Ribble.

For most of the 19th century travel between the towns was along badly maintained country lanes. West of Tarleton, travellers were able to join the slightly better Liverpool to Preston turnpike road, which was maintained by tolls taken at Bretherton and Penwortham. The journey time for shire horses between Tarleton and Preston took some 3 hours in the early 1800s. The only direct coach service between the towns was begun in 1833 by H. Schofield, with three return coaches per week. Even as late as 11 February 1888 the *Preston Guardian* reported that 'the portion of the main Southport to Preston road between Banks and Tarleton is in a very unsafe and neglected condition, owing to the rough materials used for the pavement and to the wide and deep drains which run almost the entire length of the road.' Indeed, the situation had been so bad in Banks that horses dragging loads of produce to Preston had been fitted with broad appendages to their feet called pattens, to prevent their sinking knee-deep.

Southport, on the Irish Sea coast, is fringed to the north by the Ribble estuary, and the sea is rarely seen except at the highest tides, though there is no shortage of sand! Hence people from Southport are known as 'Sandgrounders', though there is debate about what is sufficient to qualify for that name. The town is 16.7 miles (26.9km) north of Liverpool and 14.8 miles (23.8km) south-west of Preston.

Background to Preston and Southport during the Victorian era

Southport was founded in 1792 when William Sutton, an innkeeper from Churchtown, built a bathing house at what is now the south end of Lord Street. At that time the area, known as South Hawes, was sparsely populated and dominated by sand dunes. Southport grew quickly in the late 19th century as it gained a reputation for being a more refined seaside resort than its neighbour up the coast, Blackpool. In fact, Southport had a head start compared to all the other places on the Lancashire coast because it had easy access to the canal system, which preceded the first railways. Other seaside bathing areas were not able to really get going until the railways were built some years later.

In the late 18th century it was becoming fashionable for the well-to-do to relinquish inland spa towns and visit the seaside to bathe in the salt sea waters. More than 100 years before the beginnings of the WLR in 1878, the canals brought visitors and goods to the developing hamlet of Southport. The Leeds & Liverpool Canal was built in 1774 from Liverpool to Wigan, and the link from Wigan to Manchester was opened in 1820. This was an integrated canal network that brought the public from Liverpool, Manchester, Bolton and Wigan to Scarisbrick, with carriages conveying them to Southport, culminating in the town hosting more than 20,000 visitors each year by 1820. Hence Southport was already a holiday resort before the established railway network, but gained by having one in the late Victorian era.

Although there was no direct rail link, Southport was first reached by rail from Preston in 1855, from a junction at Burscough Bridge on

WLR 0-4-2 No 1 *Edward Holden*. Roger Roberts, L&YR Society

the Preston to Liverpool line, which linked it with the Manchester to Southport line. Consequently remote villages situated along the south bank of the Ribble remained isolated.

The West Lancashire Railway (WLR) was promoted by several prominent Southport citizens, in part as a tangible feature of resistance to what was seen as an increasing monopoly of railways in the county by the Lancashire & Yorkshire Railway (L&YR). The WLR eventually opened between Southport and Preston Fishergate Hill in September 1882. Henceforth funny old steam-hauled trains began to characterise the local landscape just like those in the accompanying photographs.

The railway was welcomed by farmers for the transportation of their vegetables and livestock, as well as by a limited number of commuters to the two towns, and not least by providers to the expanding holiday trade in Southport. The railway's opening, in stages from 1878 to 1882, fostered this spirit of optimism, buoyed up by high expectations of forthcoming prosperity. The first phase was opened from Hesketh Park to Hesketh Bank on 19 February 1878. On 18 May 1882 the 3-mile stretch linking Hesketh Park with Longton opened with one intermediate station at Hoole. A feature of this length was the tidal River Douglas, which was crossed by a swing bridge. The final stretch of line from Southport linked Longton with Preston, Fishergate Hill, and opened on 5 September 1882.

Right: A WLR 0-6-2T side tank built by Kitson and used on the Liverpool, Southport & Preston Junction Railway (LS&PJR) until the companies merged in 1888 when the locomotive was rebranded to the WLR livery.

Below: Stanier tank No 42439 with the 4.50pm Preston to Southport train crosses the Douglas Bridge on 3 October 1963. *Jim Peden*

Above: A late-Victorian image of the Douglas bridge. *John Ryan collection*

Below: 3rd Class carriages stand alongside the platform at the WLR's Fishergate Hill station.

Background to Preston and Southport during the Victorian era

Banks station staff in the early 20th century. *Connie Wareing*

Right: A Southport to Crossens EMU service departs from St Luke's on 17 April 1939. *E. R. Morton*

Left: Long Lane ground frame of 1909, alongside the level crossing just west of Banks station. *Connie Wareing*

Centre left: Square House Lane signal box, Banks. *John Williams*

Bottom left: Another view of Square House Lane signal box, while the staff 'take five'. *Connie Wareing*

Right: Fairburn 2-6-4T No 42296 is given the right of way at Square House Lane with the 8.58am Saturdays-only Colne to Southport service on 23 August 1964. *David Hampson*

Below: Crossens station in 1912. *Connie Wareing*

1 • The Victorian 'railway mania' and its aftermath

In this introductory chapter I examine the origin of the first r ailways around Preston and Southport and their ultimate relevance to the Preston to Southport branch line.

The impact of the dawn of the railways was being felt during the mid to late Victorian period as the stagecoach, canal barge and various types of horse-drawn vehicles were eventually overtaken by the iron horse. The evolving railway network was assisted by the inadequacy of the canal and road network and the high profits made by the canal operators. Indeed, the term 'railway mania' has been applied to an utter frenzy surrounding rail construction during the mid-Victorian era.

Railway mania reached its peak in 1846, when no fewer than 272 Acts of Parliament were enacted to set up new companies and thereby establish new railways. From a social perspective this newly found mobility lured the public long before the dawn of the automobile. For about 75 years the railways were the only form of proper land transport, and they it was that changed everything. Britain's passenger railways grew to 13,500 miles of track by 1870, rising to more than 20,000 miles and operated by some 120 competing companies by the time of the First World War.

The Wigan & Preston Junction Railway became part of the North Union Railway on 1 November 1838. Entering Wigan from the south, it gave Preston a rail connection with the major cities of London, Birmingham, Manchester and Liverpool. The new railway from Wigan reduced the time taken by stagecoach from 3 hours to less than half an hour. The inaugural return trip was duly reported in the *Preston Chronicle*: 'Loud huzzas greeted our arrival, the bells sent forth their sonorous peals, the Union Jack was unfurled on the parish church, the standard of St George floated on top of the Mayor's Mansion and a band of music played in the gardens.'

The original Preston station was the earliest within the bounds of the present county of Lancashire and soon became a major junction. Originally it comprised only two platforms, which had expanded to six tracks, four platforms and an extended station building by 1847. The Preston historian Anthony Hewitson, writing in 1883, did not speak too favourably about the original North Union station or of the first steam engines:

'At Preston the station was one of the most dismal, dilapidated, disgraceful-looking structures in Christendom. It was not only a very ill-looking, but an exceedingly inconvenient and dangerous station. The engines were said to be very small and the weak character of the old engines was such that often, when a heavy train was leaving Preston for the north, porters had to push at the side by way of assistance.'

Furthermore, passengers had to cross the railway lines to reach other platforms. This dangerous procedure was finally ended when a footbridge was erected in 1855.

Nevertheless, Hewitson noted in 1883:

'As to railways, Preston has, for many years, been one of the principal centres… No town in the Kingdom possesses a more comprehensive railway service… Prestonians possess facilities which but few provincial people enjoy anywhere. About 450 trains, passenger and goods, arrive at and depart from the principal station every twenty-four hours.'

The increased volume of traffic, coupled with the appalling lack of facilities on the original station, led to the construction of a more substantial structure. The new station was completed by the firm of Cooper & Tullis in July 1880. Further extensions were made in 1903 and 1913, when Preston station reached its zenith with a total of 15 platforms, inclusive of bays.

The original Victorian station remains and is today a Grade II-listed building, though the number of platforms has been reduced to six, following electrification of the West Coast Main Line.

By 1848 Preston had become the mid-

Left: Pleasington station in L&YR days. *Jim Peden*

Above: Hughes 'Crab' 2-6-0 No 42828 passes the closed Hoghton station with a Colne to Blackpool Central excursion on Easter Monday 1964. *Chris Spring*

point of the London to Glasgow railway, and increasingly the developing Lancashire railway network made a significant contribution to the socio-economic development of North West England.

The Blackburn & Preston Railway (B&PR) opened for passengers on 1 June 1846, with coaching stock painted in a blue and black livery. The opening was accordingly reported upon: 'The pleasure of the day was much enhanced, that no accident or mishap occurred to cast a gloom over any aspect of the proceedings.' On 3 August 1846 the B&PR amalgamated with the ELR, and by this route trains travelled direct from Preston to Blackburn with intermediate stations at Preston Junction, Bamber Bridge, Hoghton, Pleasington and Cherry Tree.

The East Lancashire line was important to the L&YR, when passenger trains working the Preston to Southport branch were routed via a newly installed Whitehouse Triangle and the ELR viaduct across the Ribble. (This viaduct should not to be confused with the original WLR crossing of the Ribble, which opened at Broadgate, Preston, in 1882.) A connection from Whitehouse North Junction to Preston (Butler Street) was installed on 16 July 1900, and from that date the original Fishergate Hill station in Preston, terminus of the former WLR, closed to passenger traffic after only 18 years, and Preston to Southport trains utilised the new route from Preston to Penwortham Junction.

The East Lancashire Line became known as the East Lancashire & Liverpool Railway when, in 1846, the Liverpool, Ormskirk & Preston Railway (LO&PR) amalgamated with the ELR, though it was not until 2 April 1849 that the LO&PR was officially opened. Moreover, it became necessary for trains from Liverpool to reverse from Lostock Hall to Preston. This and other factors caused the ELR to apply for a new independent route into Preston, and a bill was passed on 22 July 1847, with work commencing in November 1848 on the 'Bamber Bridge and Preston Extension'.

It was not until 1850 that the East Lancashire lines gained a direct independent

The Victorian 'railway mania' and its aftermath

route into Preston. This was obviously more expedient than having to reverse trains from Lostock Hall to reach Preston via Farington and the North Union route. Trains approached Preston along a route from the south-east via Preston Junction, later to be known as Todd Lane Junction, linked with the 'Bamber Bridge and Preston Extension'. The route necessitated the construction of a new and what proved to be a particularly difficult viaduct crossing of the River Ribble.

The biggest engineering work on the Preston extension was across the bog-like flood plain between Whitehouse Junction and the ELR railway viaduct. Therefore a spectacular 53-arch viaduct and iron bridge with three stone and brick arches was constructed spanning the spongy soil of the flood plain and the River Ribble itself. On the Preston side of the bridge crossing the river, an additional archway spanned a path separating Avenham and Miller parks, making a total of 57 arches.

Deep piling was required for each pier before solid ground could be reached, but apparently not successfully! On Thursday 25 October 1849 the work was delayed for several months after the collapse of 13 arches following bad weather.

Following reconstruction of the arches, engineers Errington and Meek had every confidence in the structure, and to prove it they travelled across it with a test train on 15 August 1850. The train consisted of two of the company's heaviest locomotives and wagons loaded with earth. After several such crossings the masonry was examined and found to be satisfactory and the line was opened to passenger traffic on 2 September 1850, and to goods traffic some two months later. The new line ran into new platforms built on the east side of the NUR's station, which were managed and staffed by the ELR, and which had their own booking hall and entrance. However, by 1883 sections of the viaduct were found to be structurally unsafe. A costly operation was put into effect involving filling in the arches with earth, clay, rubble and refuse from land-fill sites to create an embankment. Excavated material from the newly completed engine shed at Lostock Hall was also used.

The following passage is taken from *History of Preston* (1883) by the Preston historian Anthony Hewitson, and provides interesting details concerning the viaduct:

'It was built by Mr Cornie. Its main arches, spanning the river, are three in number: they are of iron, with brick and stone piers. In connection with them, running southward, there are 53 brick arches. In some parts these arches have an uneven appearance, and at such parts the sides have been tie-rodded. Softness of foundation has, apparently, caused the defects referred to. A public footway runs along the higher or eastern side of the river arches. When the bill of the Railway Company was in Parliament, the Corporation of Preston, who had some notion of making a public park on the southern side of the river, lodged against it certain opposition, which was withdrawn through the Company agreeing to make the footway named, and ornament, with trees and shrubbery, the railway embankment on the Preston side. Adjoining, and on the northern side of the bridge crossing the river, an archway spans the foot walk, near the water edge; so that, altogether, this structure consists of 57 arches.'

Todd Lane Junction station, photographed on 26 June 1963. *Jim Peden*

The East Lancs Bridge as it appeared in the *Illustrated London News* at the time of the Preston Guild in 1862.

Above: A Victorian perspective on the footpath that ran alongside the ELR; the viaduct carried the East Lancashire and Liverpool lines and the WLR from Preston. *Harris Museum, Preston*

The ELR's Ribble viaduct was impressive and complemented Charles Vignoles's fine Grade II-listed five-arch bridge downstream, which carried the North Union Railway. One of the conditions laid down by Preston Corporation was that provision be made for a public footpath across the river. The viaduct was therefore fitted with cantilever brackets on the east side, upon which a narrow footpath was constructed, accessed by a flight of steep steps on both sides of the river.

The ELR also built the particularly ornate Ivy Bridge with its balustrade over the Broad

Below: A different view of the ELR viaduct through an arch of Charles Vignoles's bridge. *Harris Museum, Preston*

Above: Viewed from Miller Park in Victorian times, the awesome ELR viaduct spanning the River Ribble at Preston had 52 arches. *Lancashire Libraries*

Right: The ELR viaduct had four substantial stone piers carrying three arched iron spans over the river. Work on the bridge was completed on 27 January 1850. *Harris Museum, Preston*

Walk separating the Avenham and Miller parks, which was intended to be compatible with the public park amenity. Intriguingly, because of its limited height it still has an elliptical arch on a 30-foot skew. The view from the carriage window was of the two beautiful 19th-century parks nestling snugly beside the River Ribble and overlooked on a high embankment by the awesome Victorian Park Hotel. This was opened in 1882 as a joint venture by the L&YR and the London & North Western Railway (LNWR), coinciding with the completion of the final link of the WLR from Preston to Southport, and the enlargement of Preston station.

At Preston the ELR station was accessed from the eastern, or Butler Street, entrance and was served by its own platforms adjacent to the main North Union station. Following the amalgamation of the ELR with the L&YR in 1859, the Butler Street station was owned and operated solely by the L&YR. A new Butler Street entrance was added in 1913, the former ELR side comprising Platforms 7, 8, 9 and 10.

Southport, like Blackpool, owed much of its growth to the arrival of the railway. Bills were given assent in 1847 to link Liverpool and Manchester to Southport and construction work began in January 1848, with the line opening from Southport to Liverpool via Waterloo in 1850. The railway from Wigan to Southport was opened on 7 April 1855, though it was not until 1861 that the line was extended to Manchester.

The embankment and two of the original brick arches can be seen on the southern approach to the viaduct. The full complement of arches have long since disappeared under the embankment. *Roger Roberts*

'Look up!' Stanier 3MT 2-6-2T No 40196, powering a Preston to Southport service on 1 September 1956, crosses the viaduct. *Ribble Steam Railway*

The ELR viaduct is about to take on a new look with steel plates being lowered into position. *Roger Roberts collection*

The Victorian 'railway mania' and its aftermath

Above: Ivy Bridge on the ELR marked the boundary between the Avenham and Miller parks. An ancient L&YR saddle tank named *Roach*, withdrawn in 1898, crosses the bridge while probably on a headshunt.
John Ryan collection

Top right: Class 5 4-6-0 No 44753, with Caprotti valve gear, leaves Platform 9 at Butler Street, Preston, with the 9.43am train to Southport on 10 April 1964. *Chris Spring*

Centre right: Another 'Caprotti' Class 5, No 44686, departs from Preston with the 2.16pm train to Southport on 21 May 1964. *Chris Spring*

Left: Preston East Lancashire Goods signal box, photographed on 21 August 1971. *Jim Peden*

Left: On the 25 May 1964 Fairburn 2-6-4T No 42296 arrives at Preston from Southport and passes diesel shunter No D3368 and the East Lancashire Goods Yard signal box before entering the station. *The late Frank Dean, Malcolm Richardson collection*

Below left and right: Preston East Lancashire goods yard and the station platforms are seen in 1972. *Both Roger Roberts collection*

Right: Double-headed steam – those were the days! Against the background of the East Lancashire goods yard and warehouses, Class 5 No 45109 and BR 'Standard' Class 4 No 75061 depart from Preston in 1960. *Stan Withers*

The Victorian 'railway mania' and its aftermath

Southport was first reached from Preston in 1855 from the junction at Burscough Bridge on the Preston to Ormskirk line, which linked it with the Manchester to Southport line.

The North West regional rail network was more or less complete by 1850, though with certain exceptions, including the Preston to Southport branch line. The last major railway construction project in the Preston area was the WLR line from Fishergate Hill to Southport via Hesketh Bank, which opened on 5 September 1882 in time for that year's Guild celebrations. Following the formal opening, a local newspaper reported that 'tramcars will start from the West Lancashire's station, Preston, every ten minutes during the greater part of the day (except Sundays) at a charge of one penny per person only.'

The Lancashire & Yorkshire Railway was incorporated in 1847 from an amalgamation of several existing railways based in northern England.

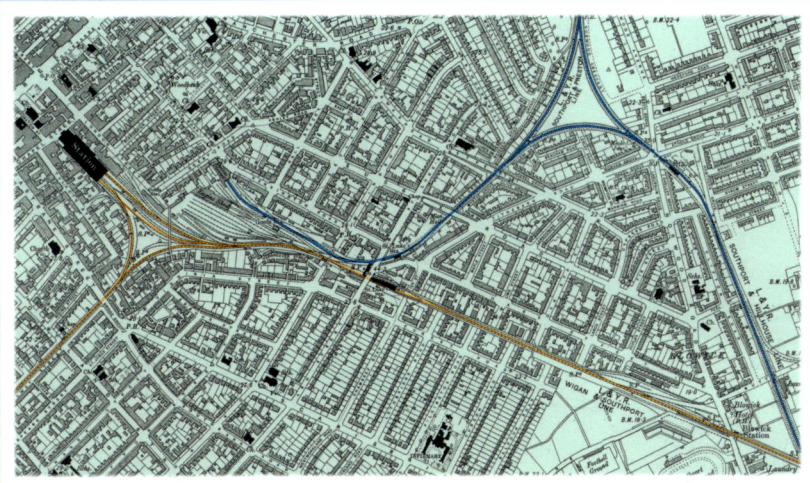

The last local service from Southport to Ormskirk is seen near Hawkshead Street Junction. The passenger service from Ormskirk to Burscough Junction and on to Southport, which used the southern Burscough curve, was withdrawn in 1962. *Arnold Battson*

Above: A map showing the L&YR junctions around Southport. Roe Lane and Meols Cop junctions (top right of map) allowed through trains from Preston to be routed onto the LS&PJR to connect with the CLC at Hillhouse Junction. *Connie Wareing*

Right: Southport Central station. *Bob Gregson*

Right: Fishergate Hill station in June 1952. *Gordon Biddle*

Below: The L&YR's Chapel Street station in Southport depicted on a postcard sent on 29 November 1904. *John Ryan collection*

The three-coach DMU forming BR's 'Sandgrounder' excursion to York on 8 August 1971 was the first passenger train out of the former Central station in 70 years, and positively the last before the station closed shortly afterwards. *Cedric Greenwood*

The Lancashire & Yorkshire Railway Act merged with the Liverpool, Crosby & Southport Railway in 1855, the ELR in 1858, and the WLR together with its subsidiary the Liverpool, Southport & Preston Junction Railway in July 1897. The lines from Manchester, Preston and Downholland were channelled into Chapel Street station following the closure of London Street station circa 1860 and Central station in 1901. Southport Chapel Street station underwent expansion with the addition of a new ticket office.

In conclusion, the borough of Southport once had a total of 22 stations and one halt, and was the terminus of five railways: originally the Liverpool, Crosby & Southport Railway into East

The Victorian 'railway mania' and its aftermath

Bank Street station (1848); the WLR from Preston to Southport Central station (1882); the ELR from Manchester into London Street station (1855); the Southport & Cheshire Lines Extension from Aintree into Lord Street station (1884); and finally the Liverpool, Southport & Preston Junction Railway from Downholland, which shared Southport's Central station with the WLR (1887). Today the five lines that served Southport have been reduced to two and the number of stations (suburban and mainline) has been reduced to five. However, the magnificent edifice of Lord Street station, which once served the Cheshire Lines, survives as a monument to a Victorian railway hysteria, albeit now the entrance to a supermarket.

The Southport, Cheshire & Liverpool Extension Railway (CLC)

The Cheshire Lines Committee (CLC) was formed in the 1860s and became the second-largest joint railway in Great Britain. It operated 143 miles (230km) of track in the then counties of Lancashire and Cheshire, principally serving stations in Cheshire and Liverpool. The railway was not grouped in 1923 and remained independent until nationalisation in 1948, while operated by the CLC.

The double-track Southport, Cheshire & Liverpool Extension Railway opened in September 1884 having been promoted by an eight strong consortium led by Walter Smith, four times mayor of Southport and sole contractor for the 14 miles 3 chains (22.6km) long line. The railway

The coat of arms of the Cheshire Lines Committee. *Roger Roberts*

Top right: Southport's Lord Street station was opened in 1884 and closed in 1952. With extensive glass roofing, it boasted a fine façade and Victorian tower dominating Lord Street, which remains to this day although a supermarket has now succeeded the trains.

Right: The interior of Lord Street circa 1910. *Jim Peden*

connected the Liverpool Extension line at Aintree to Southport Lord Street The CLC. operated the line, providing locomotives and rolling stock.

By 1895 Lord Street station had 17 daily departures and arrivals. The first station out of Lord Street was Birkdale Palace; south of Birkdale the railway trackbed is now occupied by the coastal road and passes the site of Ainsdale Beach station. Thereafter there were stations at Mossbridge, Altcar & Hillhouse Junction, Lydiate, Sefton & Maghull and Aintree Central. However, the CLC line could not compete with the L&YR's more direct route from Liverpool to Southport Chapel Street. The CLC closed to passengers on 7 January 1952 and to goods traffic the following 7 July, and thereafter Lord Street station became a bus station. However, the very last passenger train to

Left: A freight train passes through the CLC's Altcar & Hillhouse station in about 1950. The locomotive is believed to be 0-6-0 No 44318. *R. C. Chown, Robert Miller collection*

Above: Following closure of the CLC line to Southport in 1952, Lord Street railway station was transformed to a bus station. *Bob Gregson*

Below: Ainsdale L&YR station before demolition of the original LC&SR house on the up platform. *Bob Gregson collection*

Above: This is Altcar & Hillhouse station and goods siding looking north on 10 April 1954. *Jim Peden, Robert Miller collection*

Right: The Railway Signal Box Co box at Altcar on 6 June 1959. *Robert Miller collection*

The Victorian 'railway mania' and its aftermath

run on the CLC was a railway enthusiasts' 'special' between Aintree and Altcar & Hillhouse stations on 6 June 1959.

As we will see in Chapter Two, the WLR was born at the end of a period of national railway construction and was gradually integrated into the emerging rail network. Since those golden years, and lamentably, perhaps, due to a lack of vision, the Preston to Southport branch line has passed into the annals of railway history. We owe a debt of gratitude to the men of foresight who built the railways and thus provided vital links to the outside world prompting a social revolution, which impacted on local communities throughout the country.

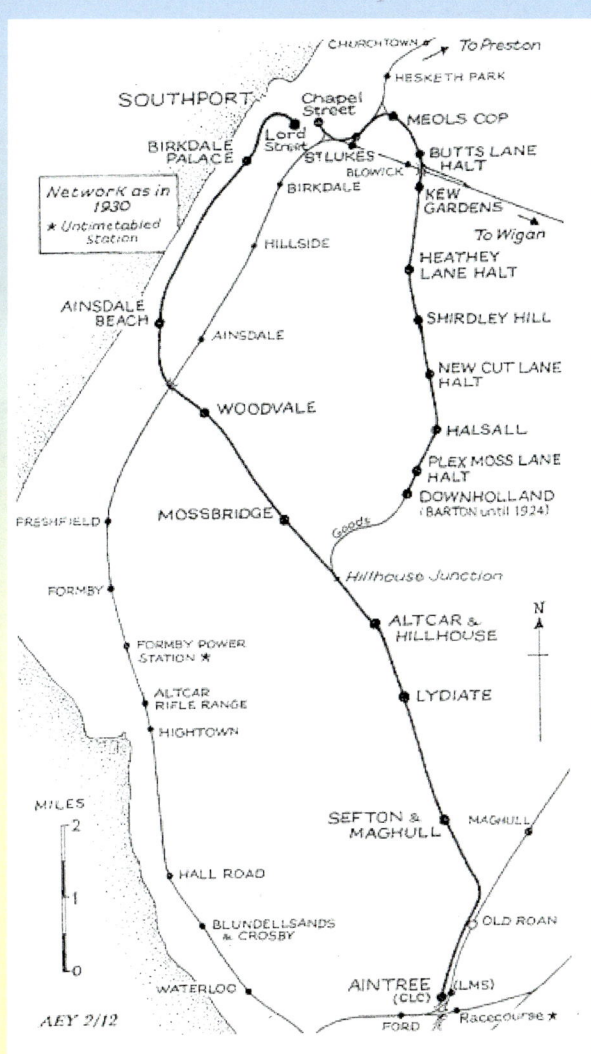

Above: Dereliction at Altcar & Hillhouse Junction following closure. *Jim Peden, J. B. Horne collection*

Right: A map showing the lines emanating from Southport and the course of the CLC and the LS&PJR (Altcar & Hillhouse branch line).

2 • The origin and construction of the West Lancashire Railway

In this chapter I examine the origin, construction and phased openings of the West Lancashire Railway, including stations and infrastructure as well as the significance of the Penwortham and Whitehouse triangles.

The origin of the WLR

Although the WLR Act passed through Parliament in July 1871, so many were the difficulties of the promoters that the line was not opened until seven years later, and then only between Hesketh Park (Southport) and Hesketh Bank.

The WLR was promoted by Walter Smith, who had brought the ELR to Southport in 1855. Walter was four times Mayor of Southport, and also promoted the Southport Tramways (1873), the Winter Gardens (1874), and the Botanic Gardens (1875). The birth of the WLR was intended to break the monopoly of the L&YR by providing a direct route to Liverpool and Preston as an alternative to the longer route from Southport via Burscough. It was seen as a realistic alternative by the promoters and locals alike, and perhaps a fitting crown towards the end of a period of intense national railway construction throughout the mid to late 19th century.

There was considerable local animosity towards the L&YR, which, it has been suggested, was the catalyst for the early Preston to Southport branch line proposals. The L&YR firmly held the monopoly of rail links into Southport. The company had taken over the Liverpool to Southport and Manchester to Southport lines and the connection to Preston at Burscough. The Cheshire Lines Extension Railway from Liverpool to Lord Street station at Southport would not be opened until 1884.

The coat of arms of the West Lancashire Railway.
Gordon McWilliam, Roger Roberts collection

Interestingly, in 1838, ten years before any railway lines ran into Southport, a proposal was made to connect Liverpool, Southport and Preston by rail, but the scheme did not meet with any support and it was not until 1846 that a bill was laid before Parliament. However, the bill was not approved as members did not consider that the population 'thinly spread in small scattered villages' could provide sufficient traffic to support a railway (Marshall, 1981: 76).

Nevertheless, on 11 May 1870 the Preston & Southport Railway Bill was placed before the Select Committee of the House of Commons, promoted by a group of wealthy Southport residents led by Sir Thomas George Fermor-Hesketh, Bart. Notwithstanding severe opposition from the London & North Western Railway (LNWR) and the L&YR, the bill progressed to the House of Lords. It was there that it failed, with their lordships taking the view that the district could not support the railway, a stumbling block from 24 years earlier. Furthermore, they said it would be inconvenient to run extra trains into the NUR station at Preston.

Undaunted by this setback, the promoters presented a revised bill to Parliament under the title of 'The West Lancashire Railway Company'. The bill included plans for a separate station at Preston to avoid the previously suggested overcrowding at the NUR station. This time

The origin and construction of the West Lancashire Railway

The engraved wooden and silver wheelbarrow and spade commemorating the 1873 beginnings of the construction of the WLR. *National Railway Museum*

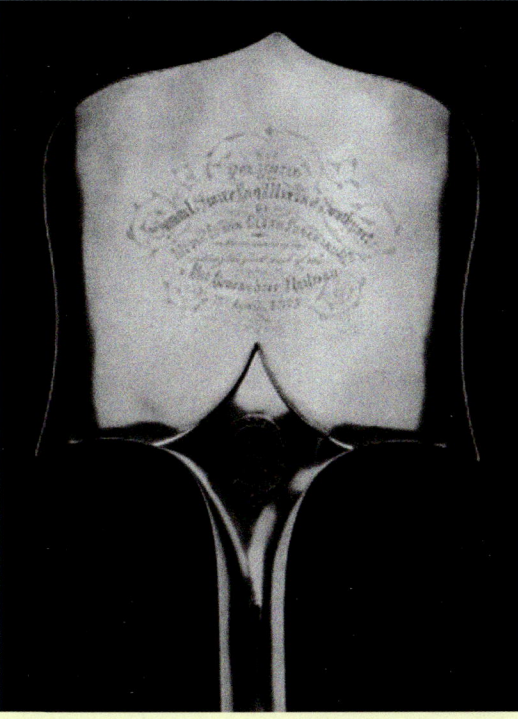

the bill succeeded and the West Lancashire Railway Act 1871 received the Royal Assent on 14 August 1871. Authorised by the legislature was a capital of £150,000, and inter alia the act laid down specifications for bridges over the River Douglas at Hesketh Bank and the River Ribble at Preston. Subsequent legislation included the West Lancashire Railway Act of 1872, which authorised links with the Ribble and Middleforth Junctions and Penwortham and Whitehouse Junctions.

The line was constructed and opened in phased sections in accordance with the finance available. The first sod was cut by Alderman Samuel Swire, Mayor of Southport, on 18 April 1873 at Little London near St Luke's station. The silver spade and wheelbarrow used in the ceremony were presented to the Mayor and Mayoress by Mr C. D. Fox, the engineer, and both of these ceremonial items are today housed in the National Railway Museum.

The WLR was designed by two of the most renowned civil engineers of the time, Sir James Brunlees (engineer for Southport Pier and the Kent and Levens viaducts on the Furness Railway) and Charles Fox, who went onto design many other major railway projects throughout the country. The contract for the construction was awarded to Clarke, Punshard & Company; however, the work ceased within months due to the financial difficulties of the contractor, and it was to be three years before work would resume.

Meetings between WLR shareholders took place during this period. Approaches were made to the boards of the L&YR and the Manchester, Sheffield & Lincolnshire Railway (MS&LR) to take over the project, but to no avail. The L&YR response to these overtures was to revive previously granted powers from an Act of 24 July 1876, to build a north-to-west curve at Burscough, directly linking the Preston to Liverpool line with the Wigan to Southport line. Nonetheless, through running did not materialise until 30 November 1878, and even then passengers had to change trains at Burscough Junction (Earnshaw, 1992: 56).

Undaunted, the company progressed with the West Lancashire Railway Act of 2 August 1875, which repealed the 1873 Act and authorised the raising of an additional £187,500. The legislature granted an extension of time to 14 August 1879 for completion of the line, as specified in the West Lancashire Railway Act, 1871.

In the intervening time, during 1876 the WLR company secretary, Mr Flynt, had a chance encounter in the street with the Reverend W. R. Bullpit, a clerk who would later be long remembered for his personal involvement in matters of local history and current affairs. He suggested that in the light of the serious financial difficulties that were still affecting the WLR, an approach should be made to Edward Holden, owner of the *Southport Daily News*, and an extremely wealthy man. They travelled to Shipley, Yorkshire, to meet Holden at his home, where he agreed to join the board and finance the railway from his personal wealth. He was duly elected chairman of the WLR on 20 November 1876, with Thomas Gilbert as Manager and Secretary.

A new contract was let to Barnes & Squire for the construction of the line, which in turn sublet various parts of the work to other contractors. These included Bushell Brothers (in liaison with Stockton Forge at Warrington) for bridges, Maxwell & Tuke for architectural work, and McKenzie & Holland for signalling and telegraph work, while other minor work was awarded to local contractors Walter Smith & Sons and Porter & Co.

McKenzie & Holland of Worcester built all the original pre-1885 boxes and signals on the WLR, and most were later replaced by standard L&YR equipment. However, Hesketh Park signal box, built by McKenzie & Holland in 1878, when the first section of the WLR opened, saw continuous use until 7 September, 1964, when the line closed (Cotterall, 1982: 8). The box remained open however until officially closed on 9 June 1968 it was last used to clear empty goods wagons from the goods yard on Monday 27 November 1967.

The construction of the WLR

Work resumed on the construction of the WLR in September 1876, and the directors were informed at a meeting in March 1877 that the first section from Hesketh Park to Hesketh Bank was expected to open on 1 July of that year. This was not to be, however, due to engineering difficulties encountered in excavating the heavy peat soil common to the area. The George Stephenson 'Chat Moss' method of floating rails on timber rafts was employed in the worst of the peat beds. An additional setback was the hard, sticky clay met on the banks of the River Douglas and the River Ribble at Penwortham, and consequently the contract began to fall further behind. Therefore on 12 June 1877 an American-style 'steam navvy' was purchased from Rushton Proctor & Co of Lincoln at a cost of £1,150 plus £150 for delivery to the site. The principal cuttings along the branch, especially at Penwortham, were excavated using this machine.

Despite the difficulties experienced, the 6½-mile section from Hesketh Park, Southport, to Hesketh Bank opened on 19 February 1878 with a ceremony at Hesketh Park station. Intermediate

Above: Hesketh Bank station staff in 1899. *Alan Castle collection*

Right: Hesketh Park station was constructed of brick and stone. *Tony Graham*

A Sharp Stewart 0-4-2 locomotive hauled the first train at the Hesketh Park ceremony on 19 February 1878.
Bob Gregson collection

stations at Churchtown, Crossens and Banks opened on the 20th. Invited guests in attendance included the Mayors of Preston and Blackburn, as well as Captain Hesketh, Sir Thomas Fermor-Hesketh of Rufford, and civic and local dignitaries. Music was provided by the Rifle Volunteers Band.

The Chairman, Edward Holden, gave a forthright speech that was critical of those who had failed to support the WLR, and offered his hope 'that we may be able to throw consternation into the ranks of the two leviathans (the L&YR

and the LNWR) and that they be more terrified than ever of the opposition of the West Lancashire Company.' However, despite the auspicious opening day and his prayers, they were alas not answered, and the WLR was in liquidation only eight years later.

Edward Holden declared the WLR open and the first of two trains drew up to the platform. The bell was rung, the whistle sounded and at 11.00am the first train departed from Hesketh Park bound for Hesketh Bank. Both trains were hauled by 0-4-2 locomotives with four-wheeled tenders from Sharp, Stewart & Co of Manchester. One was named *Sir Thomas Fermor-Hesketh*, later to be renamed *Longton*. 1st and 3rd Class carriages built by the Ashbury Carriage Company, also of Manchester, were used. The WLR's stylish carriages were said to be an improvement on its rival L&YR's ancient and unclean vehicles.

Almost four years later, on 15 May 1882, after the contract for the remaining sections had been awarded to Braddock & Matthews, a 3-mile section opened from Hesketh Bank to Longton, which was 10¼ miles from Southport Windsor Road. Part of this length included the swing bridge across the tidal River Douglas. Deep piling was required and a total of 24 iron cylinders were sunk into the river bed to a depth of 20 feet and filled with concrete. The central support for the swing bridge section was built on a circle of cylinders protected from collision by river traffic by wooden fenders. In 1913 the swing bridge was fixed, never to be opened again, as commercial tall ships had ceased to use the Douglas and the smaller canal barges had ample room to pass under the bridge. Nearby, the small Douglas Halt station was built between Hesketh Bank and the west bank of the River Douglas to connect with the WLR steam vessels operating from the pier at that location. It had no public access except by the railway or from a vessel.

After the Douglas swing bridge, the next station northwards was Hoole, which opened on 18 May 1882, followed by Longton (renamed Longton Bridge on 1 January 1892). The total length of constructed track was by now 10½ miles from Southport Windsor Road.

The last section to be constructed was from

Hoole station, looking towards Southport. *Jim Peden*

Longton to Preston. At first there were no intermediate stations, but despite that construction was far from easy. It was not until October 1889 that a station was opened at Howick, 1½ miles on the Preston side of Longton. Urban expansion led to the station being renamed Hutton & Howick in January 1898, and New Longton & Hutton on 5 November 1934. In May 1911 Cop Lane station was opened a further 1½ miles from Howick; this was to be renamed Penwortham Cop Lane in May 1940.

Again the American 'steam navvy' was used to excavate the deepest cutting on the branch next to Cop Lane. This machine was capable of scooping out 1,500 cubic yards of earth every 24 hours, and was the first machine of its kind to be used in railway construction, and was serviced by 11 contractor's locomotives.

The River Ribble crossing at Penwortham involved a lot of major preparatory work, and when finished the bridge comprised six stone piers (one on each bank and four in the

The old wooden name sign at Hoole station, probably a L&YR relic, survived until closure of the branch. *Alan Castle*

Stanier No 42445 arrives at Hoole on 8 August 1964 with the 12.40pm Southport to Preston service. *David Hampson*

Fairburn 2-6-4T No 42138, on a Southport-Preston train, arrives at Longton Bridge station on 2 September 1964. *The late Frank Dean, Malcolm Richardson collection*

This period postcard shows Chapel Lane level crossing at Howick and the small village the railway served. The station was renamed New Longton & Hutton in 1934. *Les Harrison*

The origin and construction of the West Lancashire Railway

Fairburn 2-6-4T No 42156 is heading the 2.26pm Preston to Southport service. The old-fashioned wooden sign proclaiming New Longton & Hutton is likely to be of 1924 origin, when the station was renamed. *David Hampson*

Hutton & Howick station, circa 1922. *Tony Graham*

On 1 September 1964 Stanier 2-6-4 tank No 42445 departs from New Longton & Hutton with the 7.02am service for Southport. *Alan Castle*

New Longton signal box and level crossing gates. *John Williams*

A regular on the Preston-Southport line, Stanier 'Caprotti' Class 5 No 44745 passes beneath the arches of the occupation bridge that crossed over the deepest cutting on the branch at Penwortham. *Alan Castle*

Above: BR 'Standard' Class No 75048 arrives at Cop Lane with the 6.21pm Preston-Southport service on 2 September 1964. *Alan Castle*

Above right: The WLR bridge spanning the River Ribble at Lower Penwortham, built alongside the old Broadgate road bridge, linked the WLR with its original terminus at Fishergate Hill, Preston. *Harris Museum, Preston*

Right: This is the WLR crossing of the Ribble, looking towards Fishergate Hill. *Harris Museum, Preston*

river) and five iron spans. At the south-west end there were iron bridges over the main Leyland Road and Stricklands Lane, a minor road. The ironwork for all the bridges was supplied and fixed by the Stockton Forge and supervised by that company's resident engineer, Mr Blackburn. The first trial run over the bridge was made with a heavy locomotive and carriages carrying invited guests; these included the company's engineers, Messrs Braddock & Matthews, the company responsible for completing the line, and Mr Thomas Gilbert, the WLR Manager.

The WLR was now only a quarter of a mile from the terminus. The line left the Ribble bridge on a north-to-west curve, crossing Broadgate with a substantial masonry viaduct of 12 arches. After a short distance it reached the end of the line at the goods yard and Fishergate Hill terminus. The WLR from Southport to Preston was now complete.

On 10 June 1878, a short link from Hesketh Park to a temporary platform at Southport Windsor Road was completed. This temporary measure preceded the opening of the main terminus at Central station, which opened on the completion

The origin and construction of the West Lancashire Railway

of the WLR to Preston in September 1882, when a further short length of track was constructed from Windsor Road to the permanent Central station in Derby Road. In 1902 Windsor Road (Ash Street) station was combined with St Luke's station, and thereafter Windsor Road station lost its identity.

The ceremonial opening of the completed WLR

The final stretch of line from Longton to Preston Fishergate Hill station was opened on 5 September 1882, the event brought forward to coincide with the Preston Guild celebrations being held that year.

The line was inspected by Major-General Hutchinson, who sanctioned the early opening. It was attended by the mayors of Southport and Preston, and after a reception at the Winter Gardens in Lord Street, Southport, a special train left a temporary platform, especially erected due to the incomplete state of the new purpose-built Central station in Derby Road, en route for Preston. Music was again provided by the local Rifle Volunteers Band. After inspecting the still incomplete station at Fishergate Hill, Preston, the party returned to Southport for a banquet and speeches.

The line was opened to the public on the following day. It had 22 bridges, no tunnels and the steepest gradient was 1 in 100 from Crossens up to Churchtown.

The WLR's two terminus stations

On completion of the WLR, two grand terminus station buildings became operational at Southport Central and Preston Fishergate Hill. Both termini were designed

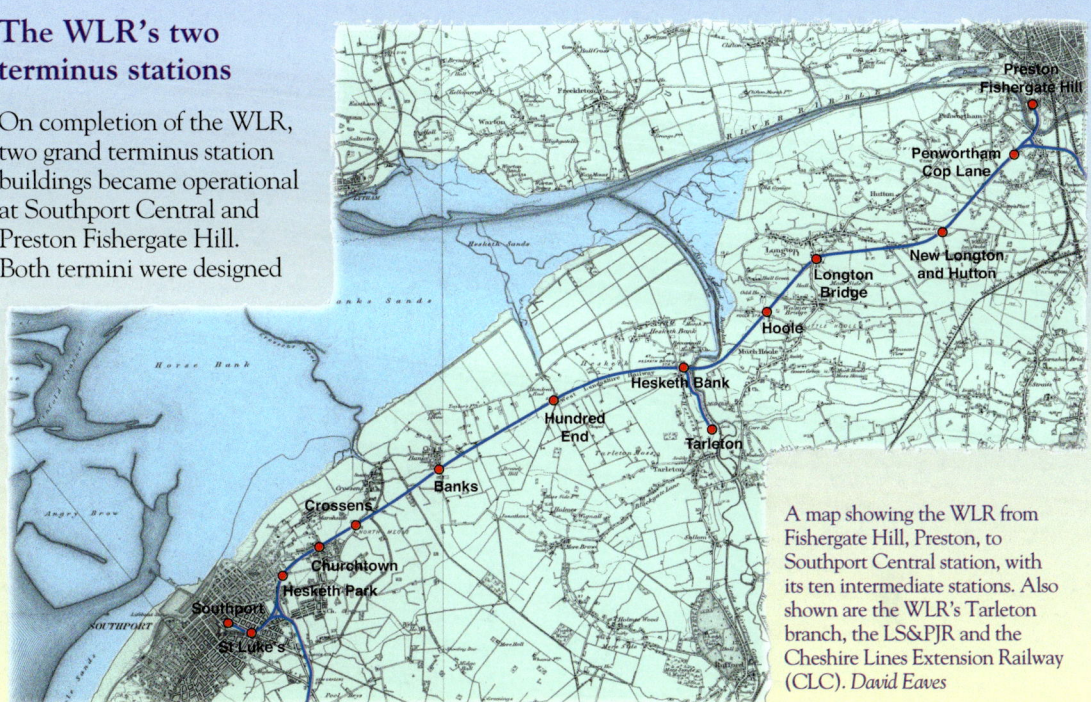

A map showing the WLR from Fishergate Hill, Preston, to Southport Central station, with its ten intermediate stations. Also shown are the WLR's Tarleton branch, the LS&PJR and the Cheshire Lines Extension Railway (CLC). *David Eaves*

in the Gothic style by Charles Driver. Fishergate Hill station had a booking hall 40 by 20 feet with a single platform 400 feet long and 25 feet wide, and was covered by a glazed 240-foot-long roof. Southport Central was situated on the corner of Derby Road and Kensington Road and had a booking hall of 40 by 34 feet with the Secretary's office on the first floor and the station master's residence on the second floor. There were arrival and departure platforms 400 feet long, covered by a glazed roof of 70-foot span supported on 27 wrought-iron pillars. It was built alongside the main WLR engine shed, which superseded the original WLR facility at Hesketh Park. After being taken over by the L&YR, Central became a goods station and was renamed Kensington Road. In 1901 passenger services were transferred to the new Southport Chapel Street station. Similarly, on 16 July 1900 Fishergate Hill became a goods depot and the nearby WLR engine shed closed with the cessation of passenger services into the station. Kensington Road served as a goods depot until 3 December 1973, and was demolished and replaced by a supermarket. Fishergate Hill continued as a goods depot until 3 January 1965, and it too has since been demolished.

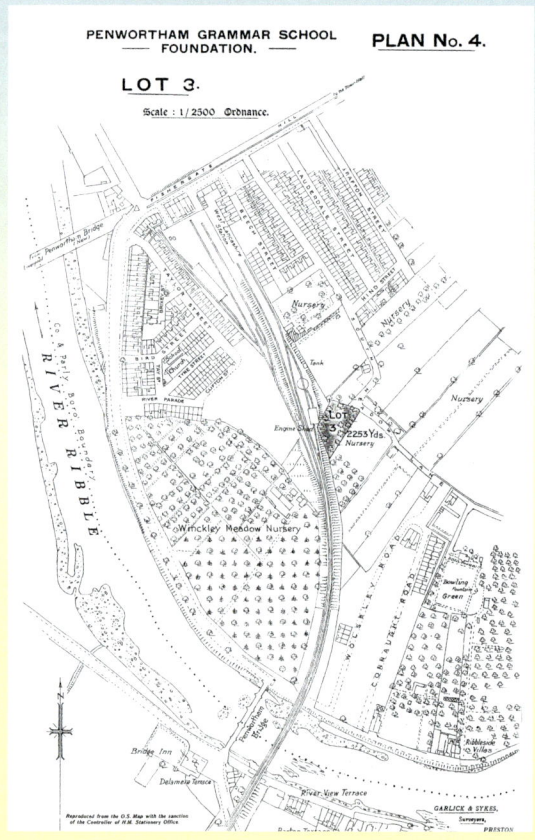

Left: This detailed map of circa 1920 shows the approach to Fishergate Hill station, with the WLR engine shed preceding the station. *Pete Vickers*

Above: The remains of Fishergate Hill station in September 1962. *Richard Casserley*

Right: Notice of final closure of Fishergate Hill station on and from 25 January 1965.

The origin and construction of the West Lancashire Railway

Above: Compare and contrast the architecture of the WLR station at Preston (first two pictures, dated August 1974) with the similar WLR facility at Kensington Road, Southport, in August 1975. *All Fred Hartley*

Above: The interior of the former Kensington Road station, Southport, with freight traffic still in evidence in in 1968. *Gordon Biddle*

Above: Kensington Road freight depot in October 1968. *Gordon Biddle*

Right: Another view of the impressive interior of Kensington Road depot circa 1970. The double tracks are now replaced by a loading bay, and on the left is a double track with a crossover. The building was the terminus and headquarters of the WLR from 1882 to 1901. *Cedric Greenwood collection*

Lament for a Branch Line

Above: Kensington Road prior to demolition in 1975. Fred Hartley

Right and below: The unusual arches and latticed roofwork of the former Southport Central station. The building awaits demolition in 1975. *Both Fred Hartley*

The Whitehouse triangle

To call the directors of the WLR ambitious would be to do them an injustice. Even before the first sod had been cut for the construction of the line on 18 April 1873, powers were granted by an Act of Parliament dated 6 August 1872 for the WLR to run over L&YR metals to Blackburn station, although this would not be accomplished until 16 April 1883, when Whitehouse South Junction, south of Preston, was opened.

By virtue of subsequent legislation, an extension of time was granted for the construction of this connection as it was clear that some serious delays had occurred, perhaps mainly attributable to constructing a bridge under the main NUR line from Wigan to Preston without interrupting traffic. There were a number of engineering challenges in the construction of this short line, but it passed inspection by Major-General Hutchinson on 7 March 1883, and opened for passengers on 16 April, and to goods on 1 June.

The service opened with the WLR paying the L&YR 3d for each passenger travelling between Blackburn and Southport (Marshall, 1969: 167). The installation made it possible for trains travelling from Southport direct to Blackburn to bypass Preston's Fishergate Hill station via Penwortham, Middleforth and Whitehouse West and South junctions.

The Whitehouse triangle was formed by three junctions: Whitehouse North and South signal boxes were on the ELR, with Whitehouse West box on the WLR close to the overbridge carrying the NUR (now the WCML). The west-to-north curve opened in 1900, allowing trains access to Preston Butler Street station. The 1900 Whitehouse West Junction signal box was an L&YR building with a wooden superstructure, brick base and a 24-lever frame. Significantly, the extensions at Whitehouse triangle opened the

The origin and construction of the West Lancashire Railway

Below: A map of the L&YR junctions around Preston. Relevant to the WLR is the Whitehouse triangle, east of the NUR/WCML, and the Penwortham triangle to the west. *David Eaves*

Right: A historic Railway Clearing House map showing Preston's railways, including the WLR's Fishergate Hill station, the ELR's Butler Street station, the later WLR station and Ribble bridge, the ELR viaduct, the Whitehouse and Penwortham triangles, and other main junctions.
Roger Roberts collection

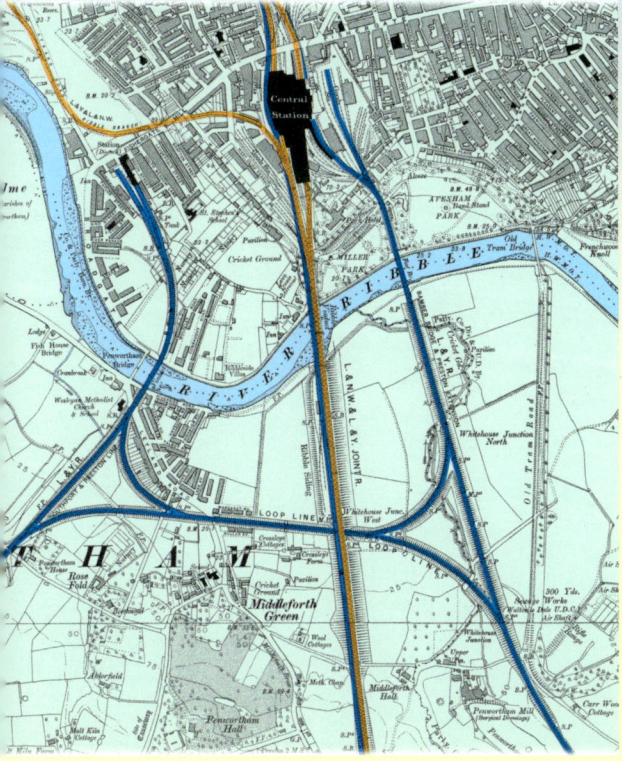

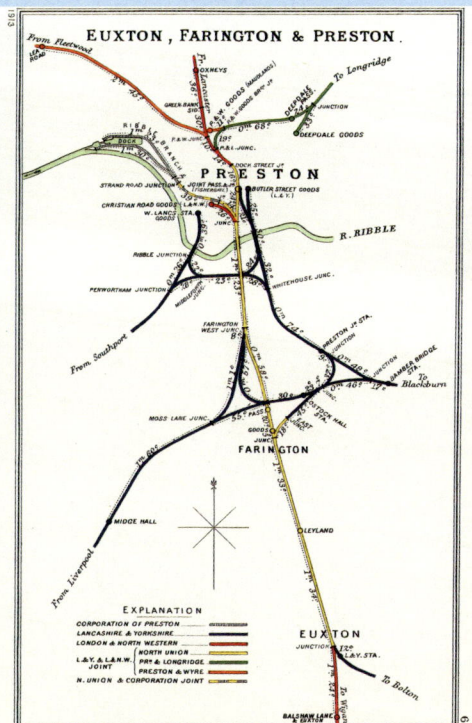

Above right: Fairburn 2-6-4T No 42135, running bunker-first, passes Whitehouse West box with a down Preston to Southport local service. To the right the line veers off towards Whitehouse South Junction on the ELR.
Neville Fields

Right: The Fairburn tanks were quite at home on branch-line working, and one such locomotive is depicted coming off the Southport branch at Whitehouse North Junction on 4 September 1964. *Luke Kay*

'Caprotti' Class 5 No 44686 hauls the 1.50pm Southport to Preston train at Whitehouse North Junction, also on 4 September 1964, two days before closure of the branch. *Peter Fitton*

An unidentified Fairburn tank comes off Whitehouse north curve and passes Whitehouse West Junction box with a Preston to Southport service. *Alan Castle*

Fowler 2-6-4T No 42369 heads the 2.16pm Preston to Southport service past Whitehouse West Junction box on 5 September 1964, the day before closure. The line to Whitehouse South veers off to the right. *Peter Fitton*

Stanier 'Caprotti' Class 5 No 44745 is working the 5.59pm Preston to Southport train about to pass No 45212 on the 5.32pm Southport to Blackburn service approaching Whitehouse West Junction on 1 September 1964. *Peter Fitton*

The origin and construction of the West Lancashire Railway

Above left: Stanier tank No 42435 is at Whitehouse West Junction with a Southport to Preston local service on 21 February 1964. *Chris Spring*

Left: A light goods train passes under the West Coast Main Line at Whitehouse West in September 1964. *Luke Kay*

Above: The view from the footplate as No 78041 is about the pass under the bridge carrying the WCML at Whitehouse West. *Alan Castle*

Above: Class 5 No 45065 pulls away from Whitehouse South Junction. *Roger Roberts*

WLR to the national rail network.

There was also a second triangle west of the NUR/WCML at Penwortham, with an east-to-west line linking Middleforth Junction with Penwortham Junction, and a northern apex at Ribble Junction, allowing access to Fishergate Hill station. Middleforth Junction box, controlling the eastern apex of the triangle, survived until 1922, having been replaced by a ground frame. Penwortham Junction signal box, with a 16-lever frame of circa 1884, controlled the western apex; it closed in 1961 and was also replaced by a ground frame, which controlled the by then single-line branch to Fishergate goods depot. Ribble Junction signal box opened with the line to Fishergate Hill station in 1882, controlling the northern apex of the triangle. All three were original McKenzie & Holland signal boxes, the company that brought signalling to the WLR before its acquisition by the L&YR.

The triangle was also used to turn locomotives from Preston; the turntable at the Preston East Lancashire station was not always considered suitable for two men to work manually. (See Appendix One for details of a serious railway accident at the Penwortham triangle.)

3 • The Liverpool, Southport & Preston Junction Railway

In this chapter I describe the rise and fall of an associated and interesting branch line commonly known as the Altcar & Hillhouse branch, or officially as the Liverpool, Southport & Preston Junction Railway (LS&PJR). It was owned and managed by the West Lancashire Railway. From the beginning the LS&PJR was a separate company in name only, and was worked in conjunction with the WLR, sharing that company's management, officials and offices.

The intention of the directors was to compete with the L&YR's Liverpool to Southport direct route, by providing the WLR with its own alternative route into Liverpool. The LS&PJR was ambitiously planned to create coalitions with other major railway companies and provide an alternative link with Liverpool and the wider railway network. It had been hoped to build a tunnel beneath the Promenade at Southport to link with the WLR and CLC at their Lord Street terminus, but this was met with opposition from Southport Corporation and failed, so an alternative plan was sought.

The LS&PJR would branch off the Southport-Wigan line at Meols Cop, then go south to serve sparsely populated rural villages en route to a junction with the CLC at Altcar. The Liverpool, Southport & Preston Junction Railway Act of 1884 was sponsored by the directors of the WLR and authorised a double track of 7 miles 4 furlongs from a junction with the Southport, Cheshire Lines Extension Railway, or CLC, at Downholland, near Altcar, to two junctions with the WLR at Meols Cop, at Hawkshead Street and Roe Lane. There was also to be a short north-south curve from Roe Lane Junction at Meols Cop that would facilitate through passenger traffic running between Preston and Altcar & Hillhouse, without the need to enter Southport.

The Act authorised a capital of £200,000 and was given assent on 7 August 1884, in spite of objections from the company's competitors the L&YR and CLC, as well as Southport Corporation. The contract to build the line was awarded to James Braddock, who had built the Longton to Preston section of the WLR. The major work involved was the construction of a five-span iron bridge over the L&YR's Southport-Wigan line at Blowick, where the foundations had to be sunk to a depth of 63 feet. Overall, in spite of the flat moss lands it crossed, the line was problematic to build with boggy ground making construction difficult. The LS&PJR was officially opened on 2 September 1887.

Originally there were five intermediate stations serving Southport suburban services at Meols Cop, Kew Gardens, Shirdley Hill, and the agricultural villages stretching over the moss including Halsall and Dalton, latterly known as Downholland. At the time of opening of the branch, the CLC line had been in existence for three years, and as there was no station at Hillhouse Junction, significantly running powers were granted to the LS&PJR to reach Altcar & Hillhouse station, a quarter of a mile south of the junction.

Stanier 'Caprotti' Class 5 No 44745 heading a Manchester to Southport excursion on 26 May 1963. *B. G. Barlow, Jim Peden collection*

This is Halsall, showing the rich agricultural land traversed by the branch. *Mark Bartlett*

Above and below: The LS&PJR's Kitson 0-6-2T No 3 was built in 1887. It was later rebuilt and renumbered 1363 by the L&YR. *Both Ribble Steam Railway*

From the 1887 opening of the line it was operated with six locomotives, purchased by the Chairman Edward Holden from his personal wealth and hired to the company. The first two were bought second-hand from the Furness Railway, being Sharp, Stewart 0-6-0 tender engines. The remaining locomotives were purchased from Kitson & Co; Nos 3 and 4 were 0-6-2 side tanks, and Nos 5 and 6 were 2-4-2 side tanks. Nos 3 and 4 were withdrawn in 1912 together with one of the 2-4-2 tanks, the remaining locomotive lasting until withdrawal in 1917. The L&YR painted these locomotives in dark green livery.

During the line's first year Bradshaw's Railway Guide of 1887 shows 12 daily passenger trains, with five on Sundays. A service was advertised between Preston, Southport and Liverpool with connections for Blackburn, via the LS&PJR and the CLC, from 1 October 1896. The journey took just over 2½ hours from Preston

The Liverpool, Southport & Preston Junction Railway

The LS&PJR's 2-4-2T No 5 was built by Kitson in 1887. It was rebuilt and renumbered 1365 by the L&YR and scrapped in 1916. *Ribble Steam Railway and L&YR Society*

to Liverpool, and the timetable confirms an agreement signed on 1 May 1888 between the WLR and the L&YR to allow through trains to run from the former company's metals through Hillhouse Junction and the CLC to Liverpool.

The WLR ran excursions, and some of these were to Aintree for passengers visiting the Grand National. On 13 March 1895 two special trains were advertised from Blackburn via Preston and Southport to Altcar to witness the proceedings of the Waterloo Cup hare-coursing event. The two trains departed from Blackburn at 8.25am and 9.23am, arriving at Altcar at 9.50 and 10.50

The timetable for services on the LS&PJR for 1906, with five new halts and worked by the railmotor, is reproduced from Bradshaw's Railway Guide.

respectively. 'It is expected that the meet will be at Lydiate on one of the three days, in which case the special trains will run to and from Lydiate station' – to witness a cruel sport! Lydiate was the next station south of Altcar & Hillhouse on the CLC.

With or without excursion traffic and regular services, it soon became apparent that the LS&PJR was not on a sound financial footing. It was never successful and not the financial lifeline that the directors of the WLR had envisaged; indeed, it was a contributory cause of the WLR being declared bankrupt in 1886. Powers were granted to the WLR by an Act of 17 August 1894 to reconstitute the board of directors and to regularise the affairs of the LS&PJR, together with a five-year 'breathing space' in which no action could be taken against the company for debt (Earnshaw, 1892: 58). Nonetheless, the receipts for the first half of 1888 showed £740 against an expenditure of £2,134,

with a further loss for the second half of the year of £1,702. In 1897 the L&YR came to the rescue of the WLR and LS&PJR with an offer to purchase, and the receivers and major shareholders accepted the offer.

Following the 1897 amalgamation of the WLR with the L&YR, the LS&PJR branch line fared no better. Moreover, the route of the branch from the southern suburban boundary of Southport at Shirdley Hill station was even more rural than the WLR itself, and passengers were few at the intermediate stations along this sparsely populated route.

To reduce overall operating costs, in July 1906 the L&YR introduced a steam railmotor service, affectionately known by local passengers as the 'Altcar Bob'. It comprised a locomotive attached to a single coach with one bogie; the driver was at the controls in the coach and the fireman was stoking at the steam end, which meant that the train did not require turning at either terminus. At the same time new halts were opened at Butts Lane, Southport, and on the moss lands at Heathey Lane, New Cut Lane and Plex Moss Lane. There were no platforms at the these halts and passengers used folding steps to board or alight from the train.

By 1910 16 return trips were operating on weekdays along the branch. There were nine on a Sunday, which was remarkable for a line that ran through thinly populated areas. In the summer of 1932 the LMS operated ten services from Plex Moss Halt to Southport Chapel Street and ten to Downholland.

The 'Altcar Bob' was perhaps ahead of its time and a precursor of the diesel multiple units engaged on branch-line workings today. The local community had great affection for the service and its crew, which was said to be mutual. Customers were happy to connect with the service to Liverpool from Hillhouse & Altcar, but only prior to November, 1926, when the line was truncated at Barton. The L&YR was subsumed by the LNWR in January 1922. The Grouping followed on 1 January 1923, when the LNWR became part of the LMS. On 2 June 1924 the LMS renamed Barton station Downholland, and with effect from 13 November 1926 the station became the southern terminus of passenger trains when services ceased to operate between Downholland and Altcar & Hillhouse – there were thus no longer any through trains or connections for Liverpool.

Left: The railmotor was one of 18 built for the L&YR between 1906 and 1911. 'Hughes' 0-4-0 railmotor No 16, colloquially known as 'Altcar Bob', poses at Southport Chapel Street. *L&YR Society*

Below: An L&YR railmotor is on the 'Altcar Bob' run circa 1915, seen with her photogenic crew at Barton (renamed Downholland station in 1924). *Jim Peden*

The Liverpool, Southport & Preston Junction Railway

Railmotor No 10605 in L&YR livery. *Roger Roberts collection*

LMS railmotor No 10601 calls at Kew Gardens on the LS&PJR in 1931. *B. Priestley, L&YR Society*

The steam engine component of the same railmotor undergoes overhaul at Horwich Works. *Roger Roberts collection*

Life with 'Altcar Bob' and the pheasant-pluckers

Despite its pretentious-sounding name, the LS&PJR became a permanent quiet backwater of a branch line, or so it seemed. Some would say that regulations were upheld, others that they were slightly bumped or moderately dented! As the area abounded in pheasants, any lonesome birds strutting alongside the track did so at their peril; some were known to have serious arguments with 'Altcar Bob' and invariably lost! Whenever this happened the driver would stop the railmotor and run back along the track to render first aid, usually understood as the train crew going home with a brace to supplement the tea menu!

Pheasants were not the only wild creatures on the menu – there were hares and rabbits too. Sadly the local gamekeeper had no sense of humour and complaints were made to the shed master at Southport. One guard was known to regularly abscond from his train at Barton by pedalling on his bike to keep an urgent appointment at the local Blue Bell pub. After knocking back a couple of pints, haste ye back to your train where perfect sobriety must prevail. The regular crew received perks from customers, such as poultry, fresh eggs and root vegetables from the local farmers. They were all on first-name terms, on this especially friendly line where everyone knew one another including the guard, who issued tickets and hopefully gave his passengers their correct change!

Goods traffic included seasonable vegetables from the rich and fertile farmland, but traffic was never very heavy and this essentially rural line failed to come up to expectations, apart from being a quirk of social history. Neither the hare-coursing community nor even 'Altcar Bob' could save the truncated line. The service ceased when the line closed to passengers on 26 September 1938. On the last day fog signals were placed on the track and passengers and bystanders joined in the chorus of 'Auld Lang Syne'. At Shirdley Hill the locomotive was decorated with flowers and streamers and inscribed in chalk 'Goodbye old friend', 'Farewell old friend' and other sentimental inscriptions. As the train huffed and puffed over the only level crossing on the line at Shirdley Hill and vanished into the night, a tear was shed by some of the train's most loyal passengers.

Competition from the road haulage industry led to the complete closure of the line, the last freight train running on 19 January 1952. The portion from Blowick to Shirdley Hill remained in use for the storage of excursion stock, but the whole of the track has now been lifted. Footpath crossings and stiles still give access to the trackbed, where agricultural land now reaches out to reclaim the former railway. Haskayne cutting is now a nature reserve of botanical interest, and halfway along it is the site of Barton station. It also serves as a poignant reminder of an ill-fated Victorian enterprise that was once a 7½-mile branch line linking Southport to the Cheshire Lines at Altcar.

L&YR railmotor No 4, LMS No 10601, leaves Southport Chapel Street in August 1928. *Jim Peden*

Five members of the station staff ready to commence duty at Halsall, 1936. *Jim Peden*

Shirdley Hill station, in 1949 with, in the distance, condemned coaching stock stored on the down line awaiting removal. *Jim Peden*

The Liverpool, Southport & Preston Junction Railway

Above left: A peaceful scene at Halsall station in passenger carrying days pre 1938. *Jim Peden*

Above: Halsall station in 1954, after complete closure of the line. *Tony Graham*

Far left: Shirdley Hill station stands in splendid isolation before conversion to a house. R. C. Chown, *Roger Roberts collection*

Left: Downholland station, formerly Barton, is seen in 1954, looking north. *Jim Peden*

Four likely lads (with six buttons per waistcoat, pre-1897 style), ready to commence duty at Barton.

Three more likely lads at Barton, ready to crew the railmotor, circa 1915. *Jim Peden*

Hillhouse Junction CLC signal box was built at their Warrington works in 1887 and was operated by CLC staff. The LS&PJR line branches off to the right. The date is 10 April 1954. *Jim Peden, Robert Miller collection*

Above: Hillhouse Junction and signal box are seen looking towards Liverpool on the same day.
Jim Peden, Robert Miller collection

Right: A distant view of Altcar & Hillhouse station, circa 1953.
J. B. Horne

The Liverpool, Southport & Preston Junction Railway

The view from Altcar & Hillhouse station looking south on 10 April 1954, showing the goods siding and signal box. *Jim Peden, Robert Miller collection*

This is Altcar & Hillhouse station looking north from the adjacent road bridge. *Jim Peden, Robert Miller collection*

'Super D' No 49434 powered a railtour of the closed branch on 6 June 1959. *Jim Peden*

The Altcar & Hillhouse up starter and distant signal still extant on 28 May 1959. *Jim Peden*

The 'Super D' poses for photographers at Altcar & Hillhouse station during the railtour. *Jim Peden*

Inspection of the signal box at Altcar & Hillhouse in June 1959. *Jim Peden*

Altcar & Hillhouse station in 1967. *Tony Graham*

A plaque marks the location of Shirdley Hill station. *Mark Bartlett*

No D2851 hauls a demolition train on the former LS&PJR branch on 15 July 1964. *Graham Fairhurst*

A bridge parapet and the site of Halsall station. *Mark Bartlett*

The Liverpool, Southport & Preston Junction Railway

'The next train to depart from Barton will be the ghost train to nowhere…' *R. C. Chown, Roger Roberts collection*

The site of Barton/Downholland station is now a nature reserve. *Mark Bartlett*

The site of Altcar & Hillhouse station is behind the cameraman. This view taken from Wood Lane bridge is looking towards Hillhouse Junction, Woodvale and Southport. *Mark Bartlett*

4 • The Tarleton branch and PS *Virginia*

In this chapter I examine two enigmas linked to the WLR, on which there is a dearth of consistent sources of material, in particular the absence of relevant minute books. I refer to the origins and the workings of the Tarleton branch and the associated paddle steamer *Virginia* – in respect of the latter, I have been unable to trace a photograph.

The West Lancashire Railway (Steam Vessels) Act of 16 April 1878 authorised the company to build, purchase, hire, charter, provide, employ and maintain steam vessels to carry passengers, livestock and goods from Hesketh-with-Becconsall (Hesketh Bank) on the River Douglas to Preston, Lytham St Annes, Blackpool, Fleetwood, Barrow-in-Furness and the Isle of Man, and to anywhere on the Leeds & Liverpool Canal, and to raise capital to the extent of £200,000.

On 30 September 1879 the WLR's carriers advertised that 'the company begs to inform the public that in order to provide for the more convenient conduct of their traffic between Liverpool and Southport they have rented from the Leeds & Liverpool Canal Company their spacious warehouse and basin on their canal.' The WLR owned at least five barges that operated on the Leeds & Liverpool Canal, and thus goods were carried by canal and railway between Liverpool and Southport and elsewhere.

The River Douglas was busy with shipping traffic in the 19th century, providing a link from the Leeds & Liverpool Canal Extension from Rufford to Tarleton lock by utilising the navigable River Douglas at Tarleton to its confluence with the Ribble and the sea. A Customs Officer was stationed at Hesketh Bank from at least 1818 to deal with vessels loading coal from Wigan for Southport, and unloading various cargoes. Customs returns from 1847 to 1851 show that almost 100 vessels discharged cargo there, and 300 vessels were loaded and left for the sea each year. However, following the imposition of shipping dues for vessels using the Douglas in 1855, trade declined and the Customs Officer was withdrawn in 1859.

The swing bridge across the River Douglas was one of the largest and most interesting features of the WLR line, but presented significant engineering difficulties when first constructed in 1878. It was built with the large volume of commercial and river passenger traffic in mind and incorporated a new Douglas Bridge station for passengers. Under the control of the WLR Manager, Thomas Gilbert, River Douglas station was passed fit by the Board of Trade Inspector on 13 July 1878, subject to a clock and nameboard being erected (Public Record Office, MT6 210/8), and notably five months after the original line from Hesketh Park to Hesketh Bank was opened in February 1878.

It is believed that River Douglas station could only be reached by the steamers, and there was no direct access by public road. Pedestrians had access from the high ground near the old church on the west bank of the river. The station was short-lived and closed after only eight years in 1886, together with the demise of pleasure cruises.

The Tarleton branch and PS *Virginia*

Above and previous page: The River Douglas swing bridge is seen with the flooding of adjacent fields and marshes during the 17 March 1907 floods. The wooden structure around the central pier was designed to protect the bridge from shipping collisions. *Lancashire Libraries*

The swing bridge permanently ceased to swing in 1913. *Jack Johnson*

A close-up of the pivot on the Douglas bridge on 13 June 1954. The Act of Parliament declared that it had to be a swing bridge to allow the river to remain navigable to shipping. *Gordon Biddle*

A rare photograph of a L&YR passenger train crossing the Douglas bridge. *Jack Johnson*

Stanier 2-6-4T No 42550 crosses the bridge on 3 October 1963 with the 5.15pm train from Preston to Southport. *Jim Peden*

The Tarleton branch

On 22 October 1879 the *Liverpool and Southport Daily News* (L&SDN) published an advertisement dated 17 October stating that construction of a Tarleton branch line was due to start on 10 November 1879, the contractors being Braddock & Matthews (the same firm that were to construct the main-line extension from Hesketh Bank to Preston), with completion set for 29 February 1880. On 31 July 1880 the *Preston Guardian* reported that 'the line is opened and that traffic is being transferred at Tarleton Lock into railway wagons.' Tarleton Boatyard Halt was adjacent to the south-west bank of the River Douglas, 15 chains west of Hesketh Bank.

The Tarleton branch was built primarily for the transhipment of goods arriving by the Leeds & Liverpool Canal and sea-going traffic arriving by the River Douglas to the lower branch of the canal at Tarleton Lock and basin. According to Cotterall (*The West Lancashire Railway*, page 12), 'It was built privately in 1880 by Sir Thomas Fermor-Hesketh as a goods line to facilitate interchange of traffic at Tarleton Lock and the new West Lancashire Railway.'

On 30 November 1880 the branch line was sold to the WLR, which obtained the necessary Act of Parliament retrospectively, the West Lancashire Railway Act 1871 having been given the Royal Assent on 3 June 1871. It authorised the purchase of land and a branch railway known as the Tarleton branch of 1 mile 72 chains. Whatever evidence was lacking, the L&YR, which later subsumed the WLR, had to purchase the land separately in 1900

A primitive crane pictured at Tarleton Quayside in 1956. *Roger Roberts*

Boatyard Crossing Halt was built alongside a small dock. Tarleton lock had been built 4 feet wider than the standard lock to accommodate sea-going vessels, mainly schooners of 80-90 feet in length. *Harry Mayor*

and research suggests that it was purchased from Sir Thomas Fermor-Hesketh, Lord Lilford and the Leeds & Liverpool Canal Company.

The branch was single track, diverging from the WLR between Hesketh Bank and River Douglas stations. There were no bridges or tunnels along the level track, but probably up to five occupation level crossings. The line took a parallel course along the western bank of the River Douglas with one intermediate halt at Tarleton Boatyard Crossing, terminating after only 1 mile 7¼ chains at a second unstaffed halt, Tarleton Terminus, the lock and a warehouse.

The Tarleton passenger train was a steam railcar, like 'Altcar Bob' on the Downholland line, and the service ran via Hesketh Bank onto

WLR Manning Wardle 0-6-0 saddle tank No 4 worked goods traffic on the Tarleton branch between 1882 and 1897. No cab was fitted, only a weatherboard, which did not cover the footplate. *L&YR Society*

The Tarleton branch and PS *Virginia*

the branch just west of the River Douglas bridge. Like 'Altcar Bob' the service had a nickname – intriguingly it was named 'Boatyard Bessie'. However, there was not enough traffic and the service was withdrawn on 1 October 1913; goods traffic finally ended in November 1930.

My undated Bradshaw's Railway Guide shows that there were six return services between Crossens and Tarleton daily, from 8.30am to 6.35pm, with no Sunday service. An anonymous article entitled 'The Tarleton Branch – Boatyard Bessie' states: 'The whole trip along the single-line branch took only 7 minutes with the railmotor running coach-first into Tarleton. The halt at Tarleton Boatyard Crossing, it has been suggested, was the smallest in England and consisted entirely of a 3-foot-square patch of concrete on the north side of the track.'

The rear of Hutton & Howick signal box circa 1905, the level crossing and in the distance, the original crossing house, still there today.

Above: L&YR railmotor No 10611, in LMS livery, was the type that worked the Tarleton branch in 1912 and the LS&PJR from 1909 onwards. *Ribble Steam Railway*

Right and below: These two pictures show the trackbed of the Tarleton branch near Boatyard Crossing, looking towards Hesketh Bank in 1954. *Both Gordon Biddle*

A rare photo (probably the only one) of the steam railcar on the Tarleton branch alongside the River Douglas. *Lancashire Libraries*

Above: The site of the Tarleton branch junction with WLR at Hesketh Bank. *Gordon Biddle*

Above: The end of the branch at Tarleton and the canal, with rails still in situ in 1954. *Gordon Biddle*

Left: The demolition of the River Douglas bridge. *Jack Johnson*

Right: Today there is little evidence of the railway bridge that crossed the Douglas, apart from the embankment and bridge abutment. *Mark Bartlett*

The Tarleton branch and PS *Virginia*

Unfortunately nothing of the Tarleton branch survives apart from four short lengths of rail, a cutting and most of the trackbed, which makes for an interesting walk along the River Douglas between Hesketh Bank and Tarleton to observe a slice of railway archaeology. To undertake the walk, from Hesketh Bank Lane turn into Becconsall Lane and pass the old church at PR46RR and proceed to the boatyard. Walk south along a public footpath parallel to the River Douglas to a stile, where the abutment of the WLR Douglas bridge may be seen on the opposite bank. Walk a few metres and the track of the Tarleton branch comes in from the right and forms the wider footpath. Continue to walk alongside the river past the site of Boatyard Crossing Halt to the northern end of the branch of the Leeds & Liverpool Canal, at what was once the busy interchange terminus at Tarleton.

The focus now turns to the shipping traffic, and in particular the paddle steamer *Virginia* – and yet another conundrum.

A failed commercial enterprise: the paddle steamer Virginia

Before we take a voyage on the West Lancashire Railway's PS *Virginia*, it is appropriate to focus on the heyday of pleasure steamers and their association with Southport. It now seems hard to believe that before the building of Preston Docks and the strengthening of the main Ribble channel some of Southport's first visitors arrived by sea. Research confirms the town's association with the first steamships as being buoyant in the mid to late Victorian era, especially with an extension of the pier to a main channel in 1864. As early as 1835 the SS *The Enterprise*, owned by the Preston, Lytham & Southport Steam Navigation Service, began to operate a passenger service from Preston to Liverpool calling at Lytham and Southport. The list of destinations from the end of Southport pier totalled around 15 ports, including Anglesey, Llandudno, Piel Island on the Furness peninsula, Fylde coast resorts, New Brighton and Liverpool. It was the PS *Bickerstaffe* that became the very last vessel to cast off from Southport Pier to Blackpool in August 1923, thereby ending the town's long tradition of sea-going vessels.

In competition with several paddle steamer operators, the WLR became an enterprising rival when the railway opened from Southport Windsor Road to Hesketh Bank in 1878. In accordance with the provisions of the West Lancashire Railway Act of 1878, the WLR purchased a 46-ton iron-hulled paddle steamer named *Virginia* in June of that year. It was primarily intended for pleasure cruises from Tarleton Wharf, along the rivers Ribble and Douglas to Lytham, connecting with the trains at Douglas Bridge station. These cruises were interspersed with shorter cruises along the River Douglas to Freckleton Naze on the River Ribble.

The PS *Virginia* commenced her duties with the WLR after a long sea passage from Great Yarmouth via Dover and Queenstown, Southern Ireland, to its new Lancashire home on the River Douglas. In 1878 the WLR promoted combined rail and paddle steamer excursions from Southport, advertised in the *L&SDN*:

'West Lancashire Railway special rail and steam boat excursion down the River Douglas on that river to Naze Point and return: special express trains leaving Southport (Windsor Road) in connection therewith. By order, Thomas Gilbert, Secretary and Manager, Southport, 8th August, 1878.'

A week later the first revenue-earning cruises took place from 12 to 17 August 1878 inclusive. The paddle steamer sailed along the Douglas at high tide to its confluence with the Ribble at Naze Point before returning to the Douglas bridge.

However, the shareholders' predictable concerns were reflected in the last of the aforementioned advertised cruises on 29 and 30 August 1878. The vessel was largely tide-dependent and public indifference and poor weather led to the *Virginia* not being a financial success. At the end of the season in October 1878 it was apparent that the business was not viable, especially as a rival ship was sailing across the Ribble estuary from Southport to Lytham on a regular schedule. Nevertheless, the vessel remained under the ownership of the WLR and the 1879 season saw her continue to provide pleasure cruises between River Douglas station and Lytham. The evidence suggests that the paddle steamer's cruises had ceased to operate by 1886 and in the same year River Douglas station was closed by the WLR.

Reports then show a change of use, with *Virginia* being used to tow schooners loaded with wood along the River Ribble, as well as being used in the construction of Preston Docks in 1884. After several changes of ownership, *Virginia* left Preston for Garston and began to work on the River Mersey and the Manchester Ship Canal, prior to being scrapped in 1899.

5 • Operations on the West Lancashire Railway

Regrettably competitive and ambitious proposals for two separate branch lines, their locomotives and comfortable rolling stock brought about impoverished finances, insolvency and ongoing conjectures and counter-proposals for the future prosperity of the WLR. Nevertheless there is a certain romanticism concerning the era of Victorian rail travel and in this chapter I take a close look at the earliest WLR steam locomotives, their depots, timetables and excursions, and the only fatal rail accident involving one of the company's locomotives, all factors that generate an altogether immensely fascinating and interesting social history.

The locomotives of the WLR

The first locomotives to run on the WLR on the original Hesketh Park to Hesketh Bank section in February 1878 were two 0-4-2 tender engines purchased from Sharp, Stewart of Manchester. No 1 was named *Edward Holden* after the Chairman, and No 2 was named *Sir Thomas Fermor Hesketh*. To commemorate the opening of the line from Southport Central to Longton in May 1882, Nos 1 and 2 were renamed *Southport* and *Longton* respectively.

In 1878 a third locomotive, an 0-4-2 saddle tank, was delivered by Sharp, Stewart, given the WLR number 3, and named *Banks*. It was rebuilt as a tender engine in 1885 and worked the WLR for ten years before being scrapped in 1895. No 1 was broken up in 1896, while No 2 was renumbered 7 in 1893. By the time of the L&YR amalgamation No 7 was allotted the number 1367, but in the same year this locomotive was found to be in poor condition and was scrapped in 1897.

Above: WLR 0-4-2 No 2 *Sir Thomas Fermor*, was later renamed *Longton*. L&YR Society

A busy Hesketh Bank station in the Victorian era. *Jim Peden*

Above: WLR No 2 *Longton*, built by Sharp, Stewart in 1877 and scrapped in 1897. *Ribble Steam Railway*

Operations on the West Lancashire Railway

WLR 0-4-2 No 3 *Banks* was one of three Sharp, Stewart 0-4-2 locomotives. *Ribble Steam Railway*

A new black-liveried Manning Wardle 0-6-0 saddle tank was bought in 1882 for use on goods traffic on the Tarleton branch; numbered 4 and originally named *Sefton*, later *Tarleton*, it was broken up by the L&YR in 1897.

The WLR needed more locomotives on completion of the full line from Southport to Preston in 1882 and with the introduction of through trains to Blackburn in 1883. Between February 1883 and April 1884 the company took delivery of four second-hand tender engines from the London, Brighton & South Coast Railway (LB&SCR). The first pair were 2-2-2 tender engines and numbered 5 and 6, but retained their original names of *Dorking* and *Horsham*. They were scrapped in October 1885. The next two tender engines to arrive from Brighton in 1883 were both 2-4-0s but otherwise similar to the first two. They were given the WLR numbers 7 and 8 and named appropriately *Blackburn* and *Preston* respectively. The latter was withdrawn in 1887, leaving No 7 *Blackburn* to work until 1890, eventually being scrapped in 1893.

The next three engines were diminutive 0-4-0s purchased from Kitson & Co of Leeds in 1884 and numbered 10, 11 and 12. No 10 was named *Hesketh Park*, No 11 *Crossens* and No 12 *Churchtown*. No 10 was sold for £250 in 1894 and ended its days with the North Eastern Railway at Darlington Works yard. Nos 11 and 12 were sold in 1887, following the decision to discontinue the Southport to Crossens service that they had been purchased to operate.

Between 1885 and 1887 the WLR ran two 2-4-0T locomotives hired from the MS&LR, due to a shortage of engines and hence gaps in the numbering sequence caused by the withdrawal of old engines.

In 1894 the WLR purchased its last two locomotives, renumbered 8 and 9, from the MS&LR. They were Beyer Peacock & Co 0-6-2Ts and were delivered to the WLR in 1895. They were the most powerful and largest locomotives the company had ever possessed. They survived the 1897 amalgamation and were withdrawn in 1914, though were not broken up until 1918.

The WLR did not have an engine livery of its own. The three 0-4-2s of 1878 were finished in the builder's bright blue, and its two 0-6-0 tank engines of 1894 in their builder's deep purple. The four second-hand passenger engines were left in the London, Brighton & South Coast Railway yellow and brown, which the WLR seemed to like and adopted for its new 0-4-0 Kitson tank engines of 1884. The second-hand goods engine was left in LB&SCR goods engine dark green

WLR 2-2-2 No 5 *Dorking*. *L&YR Society*

WLR 2-2-2 No 6 *Horsham* was purchased from the LB&SCR for £1,250. *L&YR Society*

WLR 2-4-0 No 7 *Blackburn* was built at Brighton in 1862 and purchased by the WLR from the LB&SCR in 1883. *L&YR Society*

(*The Locomotive*, 1918:1 170). The WLR engines did not number more than 20 before the 1897 amalgamation, although they were not without interest or variety; that applied also to their liveries, and most retained the bright, garish colours given them by their previous owners or manufacturers.

The Locomotive Magazine of 1897 described the transfer of ten locomotives at the time of takeover by the L&YR:

'Six of these are being rebuilt at Horwich. The Westinghouse Brake has been removed and replaced by the automatic vacuum, steam reversing apparatus has been substituted for the old screw gear, and the engines have been converted for driving on the right-hand side, and have been fitted with standard L&YR chimneys. Those being converted are six-wheel coupled radial side tanks by Messrs Kitson and Co.'

Rolling stock

At the time of the opening, 24 comfortable four-wheeled 1st and 3rd Class carriages were supplied by the Ashbury Railway Carriage & Iron Company of Manchester. There was no provision for 2nd Class passengers; the 1st Class vehicles were numbered 1 to 12 and the 3rd Class 13 to 24. Westinghouse brakes were fitted from 1883, making up for the lack of continuous brakes. The carriages were steam-heated through flexible pipes running the length of the train from a vertical boiler in the brake van. All carriages were painted light blue below with white upper panels and grey clerestory roofs.

Certain WLR passenger carriages were purchased in much the same way as locomotives – that is second-hand and mainly from the LB&SCR. Through workings to Blackburn in 1883 prompted the purchase of a bargain lot of 60 second-hand four-wheeled carriages from the Brighton company, which had been built circa 1860. They comprised several 2nd Class vehicles but were mainly 3rd Class, retaining their original LB&SCR brown livery. Also included were four

WLR Beyer Peacock 0-6-2 side tank locomotive No 8. *L&YR Society*

The WLR No 7 *Blackburn* between its 1887 rebuild with an all over cab and its 1890 withdrawal. *L&YR Society*

A contemporary postcard of WLR Manning Wardle 0-6-0 No 5 *Scarisbrick*, (the second WLR locomotive numbered No 5) giving technical specifications of the engine. *Roger Roberts collection*

Sister engine WLR Beyer Peacock 0-6-2T No 9. *L&YR Society*

Operations on the West Lancashire Railway

unique brake vans with a raised windowed lookout in the middle of the roof. They were put to use immediately and henceforth one 2nd Class carriage would always be included in the services to Blackburn.

The WLR has the distinction of being the world's first railway company to run heated carriages, with Chairman Edward Holden's brilliant innovation of fitting a small boiler into these brake vans, and piping steam to heat the train. Interestingly Chairman Holden used a 26-foot-long four-wheeled carriage for his own use, which had been purchased by the LB&SCR in 1884.

In 1893 the WLR fitted automatic vacuum brakes to its 3rd Class coaches to allow them to run on other railways. There is no evidence that they ever did so, but the use of the Westinghouse system and the introduction of the first ever steam heated carriages illustrates that in some areas the WLR was well ahead of its time (Cotterall, 1982: 17). At the 1897 amalgamation the L&YR took over 50 carriages and vans from the WLR.

According to John Cotterall, Edward Holden purchased 150 assorted goods wagons, which he leased to the LS&PJR in 1887 in a similar arrangement to the purchase of locomotives (Cotterall, 1982: 47). Moreover, the minutes of the WLR for 26 August 1892 allude to the stock purchase of three brake vans from the Bristol & South Wales Wagon Company, 50 wagons from the same company, and six cattle wagons from the Metropolitan Railway & Carriage Company.

The WLR Minutes for 6 June 1900 state that the company handed over 293 wagons to the L&YR on 1 July 1897.

The first motive power depots

With the expansion of the network, better facilities were needed for the servicing and stabling of locomotives, and engine sheds were built to serve the railways entering Preston. Ordnance Survey maps show that the East Lancashire Railway/L&YR facility was situated in the angle of the junction east of the main line, with up to five roads and capable of stabling around 20 locomotives. This shed was the forerunner of Lostock Hall, opened by the L&YR in 1882.

With the opening of the WLR small motive power depots were constructed at Fishergate Hill in Preston, Hesketh Park, Hesketh Bank and Southport Windsor Road, all of which generally corresponded with the phased openings of the line. The timber-built Hesketh Park depot was opened by the WLR on 19 February 1878 and closed on 5 September 1882. The facilities included one through road and a water tank. At the northern end of the partially built line the WLR's Hesketh Bank engine shed opened in June 1878 with a turntable on the main shed road, but further details are unknown. The Windsor Road depot was brick-built with a slated roof and opened on 5 September 1882. Details of the facilities are not known, but on absorption by the L&YR it closed on 1 July 1897. The building survived until the 1970s as an electricity sub-station. Fishergate Hill station was opened on 16 September 1882, with one through road. The facilities included a 44-foot turntable, small engine shed and water tank. The locomotive depot is believed to have closed when the WLR was absorbed by the L&YR, and the station was transformed into a goods depot, in July 1900.

The original Windsor Road WLR engine shed at Southport, seen from the footbridge. The shed survived until 6 April 1984, becoming a battery station from 1905 to 1932, a water softening plant from 1937 to 1966 and, finally a joiner's shop, lying derelict for some time before its demolition. *Ribble Steam Railway*

Fatal accident at Preston Junction, WLR, 3 August 1896

During the WLR era there was only one serious accident, which occurred on Bank Holiday Monday in August 1896. Trains originally approached Preston from the east via the Blackburn line and the west via the Ormskirk lines, the routes meeting at Preston Junction between Bamber Bridge and Whitehouse South Junction.

The following is a summary of the accident with details extracted from the Board of Trade Accident Report conducted by Lt-Col G. W. Addison RE.

The engine shed was still in situ on 12 June 1977. *Jim Peden.*

The 8.10am West Lancashire Company's passenger train from Blackburn to Preston, headed by six-wheeled tender engine No 2, was approaching Preston Junction station at 8.46am when it collided with an L&YR special train from Leeds to Blackpool, headed by engine No 1058, which was just moving out of the loop onto the main line.

One person, the Reverend R. J. Adams, was killed after being thrown from the carriage and having then been struck by a portion of the roof. A second man was badly injured, but the train men escaped without injury. After the collision the three rear vehicles were off the rails to the right. The sole cause was clearly a mistake made by the driver of the excursion train, and driver Wigglesworth admitted his error without reservation.

There were two signal arms in front of him: the higher one for the main line, which had been off for two or three minutes, and the lower one for the loop line, clearly distinguished by a ring on the arm, which remained at danger. He realised his mistake almost as soon as he had given his engine steam, but he was unable to prevent the collision that followed. They were on a falling gradient of 1 in 117 on a heavy train and would have been unable to stop at once.

The question of safety-points on the loop line was mentioned by the coroner, and it seemed probable that if there had been safety-points the excursion engine would have dropped off onto the ballast without further injury to anyone. This is a running loop, however, and facing safety-points under such conditions would be likely to cause more accidents than they would prevent.

Visually the position of the signal post at the end of the ticket platform was not satisfactory, being too close to the fouling point of the two lines, and it was recommended that steps should be taken to improve this, and where possible signals for separate lines should be located on separate posts.

The former L&YR engine shed at Southport, seen on 21 July 1963. *Roger Carpenter*

Operations on the West Lancashire Railway

A fatal accident occurred at Preston Junction in August 1896 involving WLR No 2 hauling the 8.10am train from Blackburn to Preston Fishergate Hill and on to Southport, and L&YR No 1058 heading a Leeds to Blackpool excursion. *Ribble Steam Railway*

Above: The first timetable for the WLR from June 1878, showing trains from Southport Windsor Road to Hesketh Bank. *Connie Wareing*

Left: Marshside Lane bridge and Churchtown station at the time of the opening of the line. *John Ryan collection*

Diagrammed services and excursions

At the time of opening of the first section of the WLR on 19 February 1878, 12 trains per day ran between Hesketh Park and Hesketh Bank, with an extra late train on Saturdays. Additionally ten trains served Crossens and two served Banks daily. Only four trains ran on Sundays.

A WLR timetable dated 1 October 1878 provides details of the passenger service from Southport Windsor Road to Hesketh Bank. The journey time was 25 minutes, which contrasts with a stopping train from Southport Chapel Street to Hesketh Bank in 1964, which took 18 minutes. In 1878 one train made 12 round trips. The first train started at 6.15am from Hesketh Bank (7.00am on Sundays) and the last arrived at Hesketh Bank at 10.25pm (8.25pm on Sundays). The timetable states that horse-drawn trams met the trains at Windsor Road and ran via Chapel Street to Scarisbrick New Road.

The *Preston Guardian* of 3 January 1883 advertised the WLR as 'the direct route to Southport'. On 15 February of that year the WLR began to generate business from freight and parcels traffic.

The timetable for 1887, some five years after the completed line opened, shows 17 through trains running from Southport Central to Preston Fishergate Hill commencing at 6.25am on weekdays, with ten of these continuing to Blackburn. This was reduced to six trains on Sundays with four trains continuing to Blackburn (Bradshaw, 1968: 345).

A special timetable was published for the Botanic Gardens, situated in woodland in suburban Churchtown, which opened during 1874. The gardens boasted a lake, a multitude of pathways, conservatory, aviary and gardens bursting with floral splendour and ferns of all shapes and sizes. It was a popular Victorian attraction and was conveniently served by the WLR's Churchtown station.

WLR excursion traffic

The company ran excursion trains from both Preston and Southport on public holidays.

Two ran on 31 May and 1 June during the Whitsuntide weekend of 1895. The first train on 31 May was advertised as a cheap excursion to Cleethorpes and the fare was 15 shillings 1st Class and 7s 6d 2nd Class. The train was first routed via the LS&PJR, and at Altcar the CLC provided the engine and guard. The carriage stock consisted of two carriages, brake van and two 3rd Class carriages, with the same WLR stock used throughout the journey.

Similar arrangements for the locomotive and stock were probably made for a bold excursion on 1 June, which proclaimed to be a cheap excursion to Amsterdam to see an International Exhibition. It was routed via Lincolnshire, Harwich and Hook of Holland.

The *Preston Chronicle* reported a variety of excursions over the WLR. In July 1883 St Peter's Church, Preston (now part of Central Lancaster University), celebrated its 50th anniversary with an excursion to Southport.

A special timetable was published by the WLR for train services between Southport Windsor Road and Churchtown, which served the Botanic Gardens.

The vicar led 180 members of the congregation to an 'a la fourchette meal' at the 'Scarisbrick Hotel', Southport, followed by a walk along the pier before the return journey to Preston.

Nearer home, on 30 March 1895 the company ran a football special from Southport and Preston to Blackburn, departing from Southport at 12.55pm and arriving at Blackburn at 2.00pm, just in nice time for the match.

On 6 July 1895 the Grimshaw Park Conservative Club based in Blackburn travelled from Blackburn to Hesketh Bank and return. The train was scheduled to leave Blackburn at 2.20pm, arriving at Hesketh Bank at 2.56pm. 'Four saloons to be reserved for this party, and one saloon for Emmanuel School party, travelling Blackburn to Southport.'

On 11 July 1895 the Reverend O'Brien's party of about 200 adults and children travelled by special train from Hesketh Bank to Churchtown, departing at 1.29pm and arriving at 1.44pm. The official notice to the WLR Company's servants regarding this train contained the following note: 'No passenger train must run more than twenty miles without stopping, unless fitted with a chord apparatus for communication between passenger and guard.'

On 4 October 1895 a private special train ran from Preston to Southport for the exclusive use of Dr Moon, the Mayor of Southport, with the caveat that 'a clear road must be kept for this train'. Departing from Preston at 6.20pm and arriving at Southport at 6.41pm, it was to complete the journey in only 21 minutes, notwithstanding permanent way operations

Operations on the West Lancashire Railway

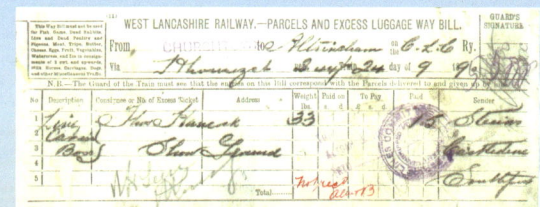

Above, above right and right: A selection of WLR ephemera. Courtesy of Mike Atherton

taking place with the painting of the Ash Street and Ribble bridges: 'Drivers must keep a sharp look out and sound their whistles when approaching these bridges.'

An excursion that showed considerable promise was featured in a press report dated 8 June 1897, which read:

'Yesterday morning a special boat train ran from Blackburn to catch the Isle of Man steamer express at the Southport pier and a large number of people took advantage of the excellent arrangements. The boat returned from the Isle of Man at 4.30pm and arrived in Southport in time to catch the 10.30pm train at Derby Road.'

Twelve months prior to the amalgamation with the L&YR on 1 July 1897 this was lucrative trade for the WLR, with 2,000 passengers travelling by train from Blackburn and 800 from Preston. Combined train and ship excursions were wound up before the First World War due to the silting up of the River Ribble, which effectively prevented all future sailings from Southport.

Right: The WLR timetable for 1896 from Blackburn and Preston to Southport and Liverpool via the LS&PJR.

6 • Aspirations, subsumption, Grouping and nationalisation

In this chapter I examine ambitious proposals for the WLR and what might have been, as well as insolvency leading to amalgamation with the L&YR in 1897, the Grouping in 1923, and finally Nationalisation in 1948.

Historically the notion of linking the railway network of Southport and south-west Lancashire with that of Blackpool and the Fylde resorts, despite the major obstacle of the River Ribble and shipping, was an aspiration of the WLR in the late Victorian era.

Perhaps of interest but not directly linked to the railway network was a bizarre tramway proposal in 1898, sponsored by the Southport & Lytham Tramroad Company. The proposal was for a tramway crossing of the estuary from Southport to Lytham on a crazy sea-going tram running on four legs on 2-foot-gauge track. The legs supporting a tram platform, linked to a transporter bridge to carry the cars across the Ribble channel to Lytham. The transporter bridge would have been 980 feet from tower to tower, and 103 feet above high-water level. There was serious opposition from Preston Corporation in defence of shipping interests, and the plan was scuppered, never reaching the construction stage.

More realistically, in 1873, with construction of the WLR only just begun, one of the directors of the Manchester, Sheffield & Lincolnshire Railway (MS&LR) proposed that the company might like to consider leasing the WLR on completion, but this proposal also came to nothing. The Chairman of the MS&LR, Sir Edward Watkin, was keen to establish a foothold on the Fylde to exploit the increasing Blackpool traffic.

A response was to be forthcoming from the MS&LR when in 1882 the WLR directors proposed to build their own line from Hesketh Bank to connect with the Fylde Coast at Freckleton over a long and expensive bridge across the Ribble, then on to Blackpool. However, again following opposition from Preston Corporation, which wanted to improve the river for navigable purposes for the proposed Preston Dock, the proposal was withdrawn.

It did however prompt the MS&LR to join with the WLR in an Act of 1883, authorising the building of a railway from Wigan to connect with the WLR at Longton. Sir Edward Watkin outlined the plan in a letter to the WLR, alluded to in the *Preston Guardian* on 22 February 1890:

'As you are aware the MS&LR, under the authority of their proprietors, have bought nearly the whole of the line between Preston and Blackpool and paid for it. What stands in the way is the difficulty with regards to Preston Docks and the difficulties and discussions about this great work have interfered very much with us both. I hope your shareholders will stand thoroughly behind you in the belief that, with Preston Dock completed, the new Blackpool line made and ultimately extended to Fleetwood and with the future extension of our line from Wigan to the junction with your line at Preston, they will have at last, with much sacrifice, a useful and not invaluable property.'

The MS&LR obtained support from the authorities in Blackpool, Preston and the Fylde to promote its new Blackpool Railway, which was intended to run from the WLR's Fishergate Hill station along existing tracks on Strand Road and Preston Docks and on to Blackpool. The WLR had obtained an Act authorising extension to the docks.

Over the next 10 years £100,000 was spent on lawyers' fees and land surveys, but nothing tangible was done. In November 1895 the Chairman of the Ribble Committee, Alderman Forshaw, told a meeting of ratepayers and property-owners that the Dock Company badly wanted another railway in Preston to avoid unnecessary dock cargoes. Also, it had expected that a bill would have been presented in Parliament for a line to Blackpool, but that the bill had been postponed for one year. In the interim the MS&LR obtained rights to run into Blackpool over L&YR lines, eradicating any need to go via Wigan and Longton. The proposed new Blackpool

Aspirations, subsumption, Grouping and nationalisation

Railway never became a reality, and the whole scheme was legally abandoned in 1896.

On 14 August 1890 a new company, known as the North West Central Railway, was granted powers to build a line for the Great Northern Railway at Keighley across the Pennines in order to connect the West Yorkshire towns with Preston and Liverpool. The line would have been costly to construct, particularly in view of the steep gradients that would need to be overcome, and there would have been an additional requirement for heavy engineering work. It was proposed that the new line would join the WLR at an unspecified point between Preston and Southport. The scheme was abandoned under powers granted by an Act of 1893 (Earnshaw, 1992: 58).

In January 1882, at the time that the Southport, Cheshire & Liverpool Extension Railway (CLC) was under construction, the WLR had an ambitious plan to link the respective termini of their two lines by a tunnel under Southport Promenade. However, the proposal was met with little enthusiasm by Southport and Preston Corporations. Although unsuccessful, the rationale of the WLR was to break the monopoly of the L&YR on the routes to and from Southport. Instead the LS&PJR was constructed to link with the CLC at Altcar (see Chapter 3).

Economic failure and bankruptcy

Thus during its short lifetime the WLR nurtured a number of aspirations that were not implemented, arguably in the spirit of competitiveness and financial desperation rather than in the philosophy

The coat of arms of the Lancashire & Yorkshire Railway.

of social progression. Disappointments in linking the WLR with these ambitious schemes, especially the LS&PJR, were an ultimate factor in the WLR being declared bankrupt in 1886, only four years after the complete line had opened from Southport to Preston Fishergate Hill. Overall the WLR was a financial liability almost from inception and failed to attract the level of commuter traffic that made other lines more profitable. The railway was in a state of poverty and dividends were not being paid to shareholders. A receiver was appointed on 31 July 1886 – fortunately one Edward Holden, who just happened to be Chairman of the WLR and the LS&PJR. During the next decade he made some progress, though it was a 'rollercoaster ride'. In 1894 a continuing downward trend became evident with poor profit margins and outgoing costs including the maintenance and reconstruction of the River Douglas bridge. Railway returns for England published by HMSO for the last year of independent operation in 1896 document passenger receipts for the completed line of only £13,839, with goods traffic receipts totalling £15,240. Clearly there had to be a change of direction, which finally came on 1 October 1896 when an agreement was reached with the L&YR for a forthcoming amalgamation.

At a meeting of the directors and shareholders held in January 1897, it was announced that the fortunes of the WLR were improving, with a net profit of £2,150. Nevertheless, there was a significant matter to discuss at the same meeting, when the Chairman informed those present:

'Since the last meeting important negotiations have been entered into with the L&YR Company and they have resulted in an agreement whereby that company undertakes certain important obligations in connection with the WLR. The new arrangements will in the judgement of the directors be not merely beneficial to the WLR but will provide greater facilities for the public that can otherwise have been given by the WLR Company without a large expenditure of capital.'

Amalgamation with the Lancashire & Yorkshire Railway

By virtue of Section 62 of the L&YR Act of 15 July 1897, the WLR Company was vested in the L&YR Company as from 1 July of that year, without any deed or conveyance, and would from that date cease to exist. Opposition to the takeover from the Cheshire Lines Committee (CLC) was withdrawn when the L&YR offered to pay £1,500 per annum for the loss of the Liverpool to Preston traffic.

The take-over by the company's competitor formally ended 19 years of independence of the WLR and its subsidiary company. One of the first acts of the L&YR

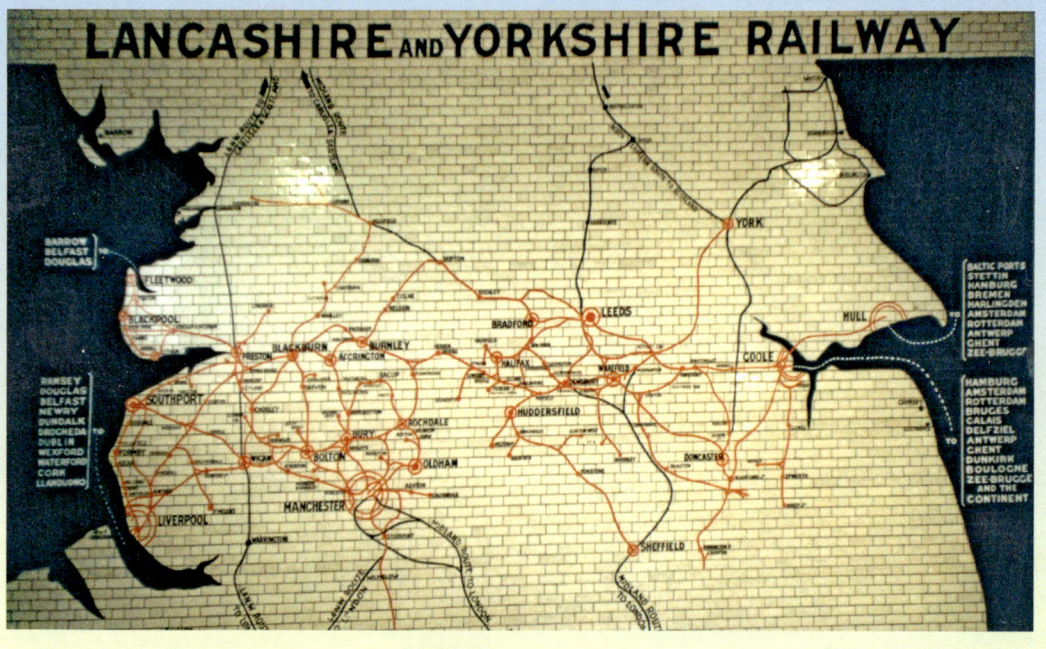

The historic tiled map in the foyer at Manchester Victoria, showing the L&YR network.

Hesketh Bank station is busy with passengers awaiting an arriving L&YR Southport-bound train. Judging by the ladies' smart, fashionable white dresses, the date is late 19th/early 20th century.
John Ryan collection

Right: An L&YR 4-4-0, LMS No 10110, departs from Southport in August 1932.
Roger Roberts collection

Aspirations, subsumption, Grouping and nationalisation

Former L&YR 4-4-0 Aspinall No 10169 at Preston's East Lancashire and Southport platforms in July 1927.
Roger Roberts collection

was to obtain powers under an Act dated 1 July 1898 to build a connection from Penwortham Junction to the former ELR line at Whitehouse North Junction to enable direct running into Preston via the ELR viaduct spanning the Ribble and into the East Lancashire's Butler Street station, which opened on 16 July 1900 (see Chapter 2). Thereafter, until closure of the branch in 1964, Southport trains departed from the former ELR platforms at Butler Street, and the WLR's Fishergate Hill station was closed, serving as a goods station until 1965, and demolished in 1985.

The relevant L&YR Minutes record that, at the time that the WLR was subsumed, it was left in poor shape:

13 July 1897: Relaying of 16 miles of WLR track necessary immediately plus 11,000 sleepers; the relaying of 25¾ miles over the next two years if the line is to be used by fast trains, as it has been since the 1 July 1897. The Tarleton branch is in thoroughly bad condition and will have to be relaid. The LS&PJR does not require relaying at present.

8 September 1898: Proposed closure of the Tarleton branch on 31 December 1898 – Leeds & Liverpool Company have no objection. The line may be kept open by running one engine a year on it.

12 October 1898: Decision on closure of the Tarleton branch deferred.

10 January 1899: Nineteen miles 4 chains of the WLR have been relaid up to the end of 1898. Eleven miles 44 chains to be relaid in 1899 at a cost of £12,705. Also additional repairs including the renewal of sleepers in sidings, buffer stops, fencing, level crossing gates and drainage of the permanent way. More substantial work involves the renewal of the timber platform at Churchtown station; strengthening of the road bridge between Hesketh Park and Churchtown; reconstruction of the sluice bridge near Hesketh Park station; renewal of the fender piles on the River Douglas swing bridge plus other repairs, total £15,102. A number of signalling plans are with the general manager and extensive signal repairs amount to £4,630. Heavy repairs to the Ribble viaduct, Preston, costing £930; LS&PJR to be re-sleepered, cost £10,387. Additional work on the LS&PJR required.

21 February 1899: New station master's house required at Banks (£253 sanctioned).

24 April 1899: Proposed alterations to station building at Southport (approved at £2,864).

11 April 1900: Proposed lengthening of platforms and provision of a shunting neck at Longton Bridge, cost £1,860.

6 November 1901: General Manager reported that as the two stations at St Luke's and Ash Street are practically joined together, the station should be combined and renamed St Luke's.

12 October 1904: Proposed goods yard at Hutton and Howick sanctioned at £1,150.

13 June 1906: Railmotor to commence running from Southport to Altcar with effect from 1 July 1906.

And to end on a sad note:

13 July 1909: Alice Hunter, aged 2 years, fatally injured at Long Lane level crossing, Banks.

The Railway Signal Company did not signal the WLR after the 1897 takeover by the L&YR, although it did supply the signal boxes at Roe Lane Junction and the original (1887-1900) at Hawkshead Street Junction, but this was part of its 1887 contract with the LS&PJR rather than the WLR. The RSC only had one signalling contract with the WLR, which was

Above: Hundred End signal box (Railway Signal Co. No 598 of 1895) and level crossing, looking towards Preston on 2 September 1964. *The late Frank Dean, Malcolm Richardson collection*

Left: Longton Bridge signal box opened in 1926. *Tony Graham*

Above left: Hesketh Bank signal box, photographed on 7 April 1958. *Tony Graham*

Above: Banks signal box. *Adrian Vaughan, Tony Graham collection*

Left: Hesketh Park signal box was an original McKenzie & Holland box built in 1878, which became L&YR No 601. It is seen on the day it closed, 7 September 1964, following departure of the last passenger train the previous night. *Arnold Battson*

Left: The unusual St Luke's signal box on stilts. *Jim Peden*

Aspirations, subsumption, Grouping and nationalisation

Signalling at St Luke's station, Southport, on 8 August 1964. *David Hampson*

for Hundred End signal box and all associated signalling; McKenzie & Holland had refused to do any more signalling for the WLR, so the RSC was selected. From 1897 to 1904 all new signal boxes on the WLR were to the L&YR's own 1890 design, and an L&YR ground-level box was erected at Long Lane in 1909. In 1926 the LMS replaced Longton Bridge signal box with an LNWR design (standard between 1923 and 1929), and in 1935 Hesketh Bank box was replaced by one to a standard LMS design. Southport Central station was closed to passengers on 1 May 1901 and used thereafter for goods, with all passenger trains running into the L&YR's large Chapel Street station. The company completed a remodelling of the approach lines to Central to allow trains to divert onto the Manchester to Southport line and into Chapel Street. Southport Central station, latterly Kensington Road, closed as a good depot in 1973 and lay empty until demolition in the mid-1980s.

A signalman at work in St Luke's signal box. *Jim Peden*

The L&YR's 'Southport Station Box'.

While it is clear that the L&YR did not make life easy for the WLR and the LS&PJR, as a company it was fourth in size in the pre-Grouping era in terms of the number of locomotives owned, if only occupying 11th place in miles of track. It introduced the country's first electro-pneumatic signalling at Bolton in 1903 and later at Southport Chapel Street. The company's unique model signalling training layout was used for more than 70 years and survives to this day in the National Railway Museum at York.

Meols Cop triangle and the EMUs

Commensurate with the expansion and development of suburban north Southport, the Crossens electric train service served the growing population. Dick, Kerr of Preston was the main contractor for the installation of electrical equipment, overseeing the transition from steam to electric traction on the Liverpool to Southport line, together with the 3-mile section of line from Southport to Crossens. Sir John Aspinall was the main protagonist in the early electrification of the railway network, and notably the L&YR held the distinction of being the first main line in the country to be electrified when the service commenced on 13 May 1904. The railway had an electrical supply of 600V dc, electric traction equipment, and a third-rail contact system. From 15 February 1909 electrification was extended to Meols Cop, and the Crossens-bound electric trains then ran via a triangle formed between Hawkshead Street Junction, Meols Cop station and Roe Lane signal boxes. At Meols Cop the driver changed ends and the train continued to Hesketh Park and on to Crossens via the junction at Roe Lane. Steam trains on the Preston to Southport branch avoided Meols Cop by taking the avoiding line to the west of the station.

The interior of the original Central station circa 1970, latterly Kensington Road Goods Depot. *Ribble Steam Railway*

On leaving Southport the Preston line diverged at Hawkshead Street Junction, seen here looking north in October 1964, with a Southport-bound DMU; the driver of which has already changed the destination blind at Meols Cop to read Wigan in preparation for the return working.. *Jim Peden*

Aspirations, subsumption, Grouping and nationalisation

Hawkshead Street Junction signal box in 1962. *Arnold Battson*

The 12.50pm EMU service from Crossens to Southport passes Roe Lane Junction in September 1964. *David Hampson*

Looking north, Stanier 4-6-2T No 42434 passes Roe Lane Junction box circa 1960. *Arnold Battson*

The track layout at Roe Lane Junction is seen looking south on 6 September 1964, with one of the last steam-hauled trains proceeding towards Chapel Street station, about to pass the EMU repair depot. *S. J. Gordon*

EMU No M28338M in the arrival platform at Crossens station in July 1955. The EMU will proceed to the crossover in readiness for a return working to Chapel Street *Ribble Steam Railway*

At Meols Cop Junction, seen in 1949, the lines to the right are towards Preston and to the left towards Southport Chapel Street. *Jim Peden*

This is Meols Cop station as it is today. *Mark Bartlett*

Meols Cop Junction and signal box are seen again in June 1962. The EMU stock was destined for the Liverpool to Ormskirk service. *Arnold Battson, Roger Roberts collection*

This is the view from Hawkshead Street bridge looking towards Preston on 31 March 2004. *Roger Roberts*

Looking in the opposite direction from Hawkshead Street bridge towards Southport Chapel Street on the same day. *Roger Roberts*

Aspirations, subsumption, Grouping and nationalisation

The Meols Cop Electric Car Maintenance Depot was built in 1911 by the L&YR at Roe Lane Junction, within the Meols Cop triangle. It opened on 23 December 1912, with the first electric motor cars and trailers forming 50 multiple unit train sets introduced in 1904. The *Reshaping of British Railways* report 1963 led to the closure of the Southport to Crossens electric train service, but the depot continued to service the Class 502 EMU sets until February 1970. Thereafter the depot was closed and demolished.

Grouping and nationalisation

The L&YR merged into the London & North Western Railway (LNWR) in 1922 as a prelude to the Grouping of railway companies of 1923. By this expedient the L&YR was to ensure that three of its chief officers obtained leading positions in the LNWR and for a number of years thereafter in the London Midland & Scottish Railway (LMS) (Simmons and Biddle, 1997: 271). The LNWR was amalgamated into the LMS as from 1 January 1923, and that company continued to operate its network through to the nationalisation of the railways in 1948. It was the largest of the 'Big Four' railway companies, and operated routes in England, Northern Ireland, Scotland and Wales.

Under the Transport Act 1947, the 'Big Four' – GWR, LNER, SR and LMS – were nationalised as from 1 January 1948, becoming part of the state-owned British Railways, initially as the British Transport Commission and assumed anonymity under the name British Railways.

Lightweight electric rolling stock was built in 1905 for the through service between Southport and Dingle via Seaforth and the Liverpool Overhead Railway. When this service was discontinued in 1913 the stock was transferred to the Southport to Crossens service; here the train is on the Crossens reversal point. *Cedric Greenwood collection*

An EMU passes Hawkshead Street Junction signal box (L&YR No 603) on 17 April 1939. *E. R. Morten*

Churchtown station, photographed on 17 April 1939, with EMU No 28696. *E. R. Morten*

This EMU, seen outside the Maintenance Depot, was built in 1939 by the LMS at Derby, and is here painted in BR blue livery. *Cedric Greenwood collection*

Old and the new electric multiple units outside Meols Cop Maintenance Depot on 25 October 1967 including a withdrawn Lancaster-Morecambe EMU and the stored Tyneside baggage car No M68000 both having been taken out of service in 1966. *Jim Peden, B. G. Barlow collection*

The exterior of the Maintenance Depot in January 1969. The building closed on 14 February 1970. *Dick Williams, Cedric Greenwood collection*

EMU No 29868 is seen at Southport Chapel Street platform 3 working a Liverpool Exchange suburban service in British Railways days. *Roger Roberts collection*

Aspirations, subsumption, Grouping and nationalisation

EMU No M28343M is pictured between Churchtown and Hesketh Park on 2 September 1964, just days prior to the cessation of services on the branch. *Ribble Steam Railway*

An EMU departs from Hesketh Park for Southport on 8 August 1964. *David Hampson*

An LNWR Southport luggage label. *Bob Gregson*

L&YR 2-4-0 express engine No 458 at Southport. *L&YR Society*

LMS No 10412 departs from Preston on an unknown date. *Roger Roberts collection*

LMS 0-6-0 No 4198 departs from Southport Chapel Street with a train for Accrington on 18 August 1939. *Roger Carpenter collection*

The coat of arms of the LMS.

Lament for a Branch Line

A former L&YR 4-4-0, LMS No 10108, arrives at Southport Chapel Street in 1929. *Roger Carpenter collection*

LMS 2-4-2 Radial tank No 10949 is seen at Chapel Street on a wet morning in 1931 with a rake of LMS passenger stock. *E. R. Morten*

A happy group of women working on the Southport branch during the Second World War. *Connie Wareing*

'Tickets please!' A selection of tickets and labels from the Preston–Southport branch spanning LNWR, LMS and BR days. *Alan Castle*

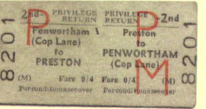
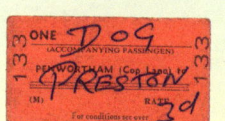

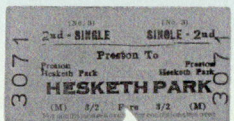
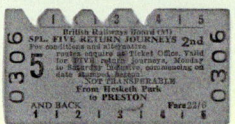
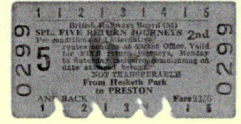

Aspirations, subsumption, Grouping and nationalisation

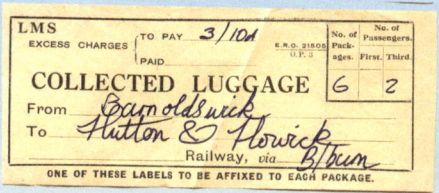

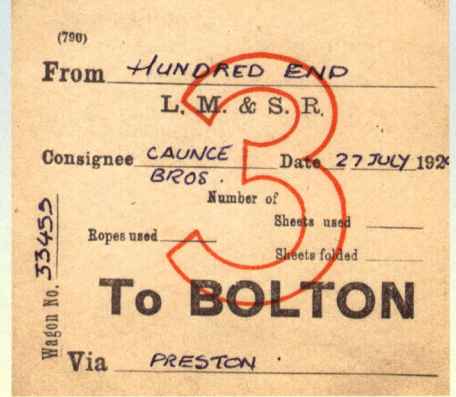

Above: BR days at Southport: Stanier Class 5 No 44728 is on shed at Southport MPD circa 1960. *Keith Miles via Peter Rigby*

Below: A trio of simmering locomotives being prepared for the road at Southport MPD. *Keith Miles via Peter Rigby*

Above: Turnaround for ex-LMS No 42548 at Southport (27C), its home shed. *Keith Miles via Peter Rigby*

Below: Stanier Class 5 No 45369 undergoes basic maintenance between duties. *Keith Miles via Peter Rigby*

Derby Road MPD, Southport

Derby Road engine shed opened in 1890 under the ownership of the L&YR. It was given the shed code 23C by the LMS, and 27C by British Railways. Derby Road shed closed completely in 1966, prior to the withdrawal of steam traction on the British Railways network, and became 'Steamport' museum for a period, but has now been demolished.

Steam locomotive allocations to Derby Road MPD included those typically used on the Preston to Southport branch: Stanier Class 5MT 4-6-0s, including Caprotti valve gear engines Nos 44686 and 44687, Ivatt and Stanier 3MT 2-6-2Ts, Fairburn, Stanier and Fowler 2-6-4 tanks, and the last of the powerful Aspinall Class 2P 2-4-2s, which were latterly assigned to shunting and station pilot duties at Southport.

Above: Ready for the day's work is ex-LMS Stanier 2-6-4 No 42637 – is the diagram Preston, Wigan or Manchester? *Keith Miles via Peter Rigby*

Above: Ex-works Stanier Class 5 'Caprotti' No 44745 stands outside Southport MPD. *Arnold Battson*

Right: Fowler 2-6-4T No 42374 is seen at St Luke's on 12 July 1965. *Jim Peden, B. G. Barlow collection*

Right: The same locomotive pauses outside the shed at Southport on 18 July 1965. *Jim Peden, B. G. Barlow collection*

Aspirations, subsumption, Grouping and nationalisation

Above: Fowler No 42369 is on Southport station pilot duty on 18 May 1964. *Jim Peden, B. G. Barlow collection*

Right: Away from its home shed, veteran 'Compound' 4-4-0 No 41186 is set to depart from Preston station in October 1956 with a train for Southport. *Ribble Steam Railway*

Below: Riddles 2MT 2-6-0 is on special duties with the breakdown train at Southport on 14 October 1961. *Jim Peden, B. G. Barlow collection*

The end is nigh for Derby Road MPD, latterly 'Steamport'.

I am reminded that as a youngster trainspotting at the local engine shed, my modus operandi was to take a quick discreet look along the shed roads, hastily jotting down the numbers but at the same time keeping a ceaseless watch for the shed foreman bellowing 'Clear off!' Fortunately this level of mischievous propensity was usually tolerated, long before the days of risk assessment and health and safety legislation.

Freight traffic

Goods traffic on the WLR commenced in 1883. In the halcyon days of the LMS the branch continued to serve mainly the arable farming industry, and there were six stations with the normal freight facilities. In 1960 British Railways announced the withdrawal of freight facilities at Hundred End, and elsewhere along the line market gardeners and farmers had found road haulage to be a cheaper and quicker alternative to rail. The goods depots at Fishergate Hill, Preston, and Kensington Road, Southport, both capitulated to closure too. By 1960 freight traffic had become increasingly sparse, with about one train a day travelling from Wigan Wallgate to Southport. The working freight timetable for the period 17 June to 8 September 1963 shows that goods trains served the stations along the line with freight facilities at New Longton & Hutton, Longton Bridge, Hoole, Hesketh Bank, Hesketh Park, Hundred End, Banks and Crossens. The accompanying plans (courtesy of David Eaves) indicate the layout of stations with freight facilities.

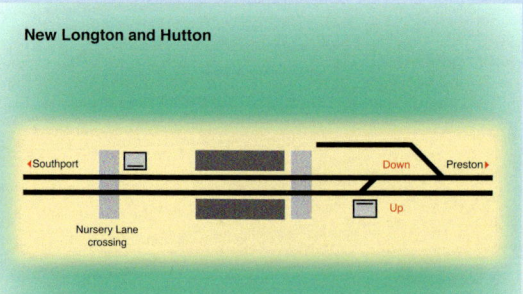

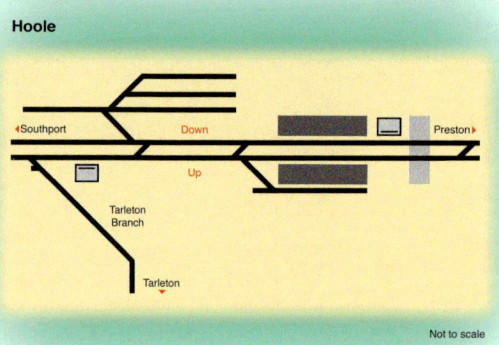

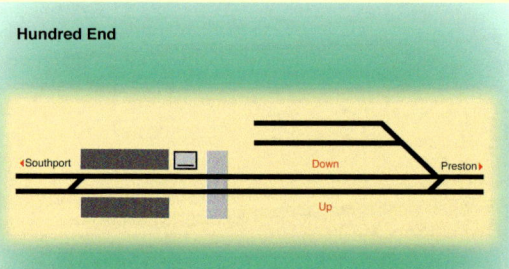

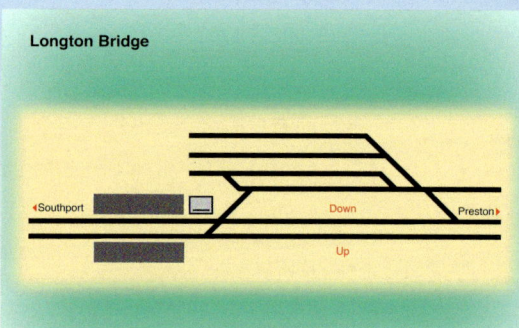

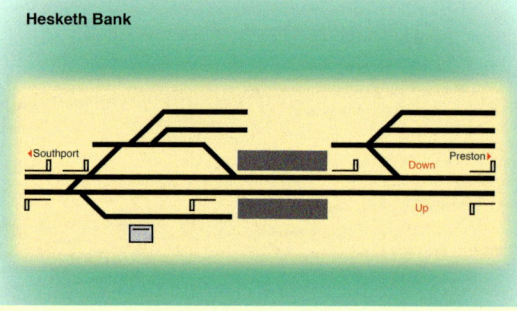

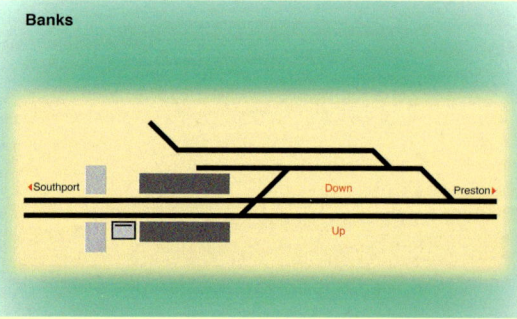

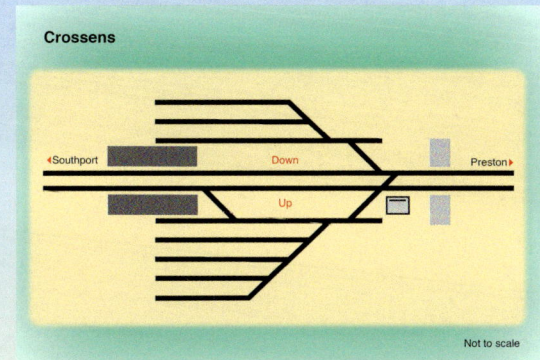

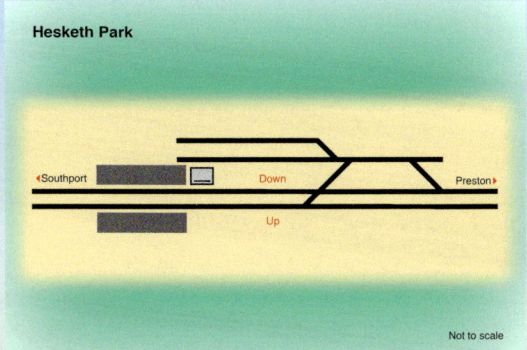

Above: WD Austerity 2-8-0 No 90675 heads the 9.00am empty coal wagon goods from Southport to Lostock Hall sidings through Churchtown station in 1964. *Keith Hick*

British Railways steam at home on the branch

Steam reigned supreme on the branch, without infiltration of the new diesels, right up until closure of the line in 1964. Following nationalisation in 1948 a range of locomotives from Lostock Hall and Southport MPDs were diagrammed to work the branch, including 2-6-4Ts and Stanier Class 5 4-6-0s. In the 1950s BR 'Standard' Class 4MT 4-6-0s and Riddles 2MT 2-6-0s were introduced. In this selection of photographs of typical workings we also take in the view of the branch from the footplate of No 78041 on 6 September 1964, together with Alan Castle.

Right: No 44757 runs between Churchtown and Hesketh Park with a Southport-Preston service in the spring of 1964 – complete with a cheery wave from the engine driver. *Keith Hick*

Seen from the footplate of No 78041, the 1.17pm train from Southport is about to cross Lindle Lane crossing on Sunday 6 September 1964. *Alan Castle*

Fairburn No 42675 with the Saturdays-only Preston to Southport service arrives at Hoole on 8 August 1964. *David Hampson*

Another footplate shot from No 78041 on the Southport to Preston service as it passes Fairburn tank No 42296 at Crossens on 6 September 1964. *Alan Castle*

Photographed from the carriage window, a 2-6-4T is travelling between Hesketh Bank and Hoole and is about to pass a Southport-bound train. Note Alty's brickworks chimney. *Alan Castle*

Clean Class 5 No 44933 departs from St Luke's. Nowadays there is little evidence of this station having been here. *Arnold Battson*

A Preston to Southport train leaves Hesketh Park station on Saturday 5 September 1964, the day before closure of the line, and 86 years since it opened. *Alan Castle*

Aspirations, subsumption, Grouping and nationalisation

Above: Once again seen from the footplate of 'Standard' No 78041, the train is about to travel the Whitehouse curve from Whitehouse West Junction. *Alan Castle*

Right: Fairburn 2-6-4T No 42286 runs light in the down direction at Whitehouse Junction on 8 August 1964. *The late Frank Dean, Malcolm Richardson collection*

Above: Fairburn No 42061 stands at Southport ready to depart with the 12.40pm train to Preston on 11 August 1964. *Chris Spring*

Right: Fairburn No 42278 is at Preston with stock for the 1.28pm service to Southport on 30 March 1964. *Chris Spring*

On 10 April 1964 'Caprotti' Class 5 4-6-0 No 44753 enters Platform 8 at Preston with the 1.50pm train from Southport. *Chris Spring*

Ivatt 2-6-0 No 46416 arriving at Preston from Southport on 24 July 1950. *Harold Boulter*

'Caprotti' Class 5 No 44745 stops at Hesketh Bank on 22 August 1964 while working the 12.18pm Southport to Preston service. *Ribble Steam Railway*

Stanier No 42645 is seen at New Longton on 2 March 1963 working the 11.30am train from Preston to Southport. *Chris Spring*

A close-up of Stanier Class 5 No 44767 at Preston's Platform 12 about to depart for Southport with the 2.12pm service on 11 July 1964. *Peter Fitton*

Aspirations, subsumption, Grouping and nationalisation

Left: Another view of No 44767 departing from Crossens with the 11.18am Southport to Preston service on 8 August 1964. *David Hampson*

Above: 'Caprotti' Class 5 No 44745 approaches to Lindle Lane crossing with a Southport-bound train. *Alan Castle*

Left: At Hoole station BR 'Standard' 4-6-0 No 75017 has charge of a Preston-bound train.
Ribble Steam Railway

Right: Assigned to the Southport line at Preston station in October 1959 are Stanier 3MT 2-6-2T No 40145 and 'Standard' Class 4 No 75045.
Arnold Battson

Above: Stanier 2-6-4T No 42626 works the 4.26pm Preston to Southport train, passing a Crossens-bound EMU at Hawkshead Street on 1 June 1964. *Ribble Steam Railway*

Above right: Fairburn 2-6-4T No 42292 coasts into Chapel Street with a Preston to Southport service.
Keith Miles via Peter Rigby

Right: Fairburn tank, No 42299, provides an interesting foreground to Southport Chapel Street.
Keith Miles via Peter Rigby

7 • 'All stations to Southport'

'The train now standing at Platform 10 is for all stations to Southport, calling at Penwortham Cop Lane, New Longton & Hutton, Longton Bridge, Hoole, Hesketh Bank, Hundred End, Banks, Crossens, Churchtown, Hesketh Park, St Luke's and Southport Chapel Street.'

This chapter describes the journey from Preston to Southport by train, together with the topography, structures, stations and the overall appeal of the former WLR branch line. I remember it with profound affection, not least for its quaint country stations that ultimately led me to the south-west Lancashire seaside resort of Southport. In later years I changed from the steam-hauled train branch at Southport for an electric train to Ainsdale to explore the nature reserves of the Sefton coast, where sand lizards and natterjack toads were much commoner than they are nowadays.

As was to be expected on such a rural line, the station buildings were small and typically presented in an attractive style of red-brick architecture, and the station was under the personal supervision of a station master and his staff. Integral to the stations were goods sheds and sidings, coal yards, quaint signal boxes, semaphore signals and even original wooden station nameboards and notices from the old companies warning the public not to trespass. There was little or no electric power and the buildings were for the most part illuminated by either gas or oil lanterns right up to the end.

Preston

Looking back to the 'Swinging Sixties', the platform indicator at Preston station shows that the 9.43am train to Southport awaits passengers and is ready to depart from Platform 10. So without further ado let us embark on the train, with Fairburn tank No 42296 up front, for both a guided tour of the branch and a mystical journey of yesteryear! We board a single compartment and admire the paintings of C. Hamilton Ellis, designed to attract passengers and excursionists to visit both local and far-flung places. One such picture depicts the WLR locomotive No 7 *Blackburn* bound for Southport.

In the meantime the slamming of carriage doors, the waving of the green flag and the responsive hoot of the engine's whistle, together with the distinct smell of steam and the progressive roar of the exhaust, together with squealing wheel flanges, absorbs all of our senses.

A 1951 carriage print from a non-corridor coach by Cuthbert Hamilton Ellis of WLR No 7 *Blackburn* on its way to Southport.

Fairburn No 42298 is ready to depart from Preston with the 5.00pm express service to Southport in 1960. *Arnold Battson*

Above: Stanier No 42551, seen at Preston East Lancs, waits to haul the Glasgow to Southport portion of a train from Preston on 11 July 1964. *Peter Fitton*

Left: With driver at the ready, No 42369 is ready to depart with the 5.59pm train for Southport in August 1964. *Ribble Steam Railway*

Following departure on our nostalgic journey to Southport, the train passes under Vicar's Bridge and over Ivy Bridge, straddling the picturesque Avenham and Miller parks, and crosses over the ELR viaduct high above the River Ribble. After a short distance we veer off right to commence the Southport branch proper at Whitehouse North Junction to negotiate the Whitehouse triangle, then pass Middleforth and Penwortham junctions to enter a deep and wide cutting on the approach to Cop Lane station.

'All stations to Southport'

Another regular at Platform 12 was No 42558, ready to depart with the 2.34pm service to Southport on Sunday 26 July 1964. *Peter Fitton*

A departing Preston to Southport train is given the road ahead, to pass beneath Vicar's Bridge.

Above: In May 1964 the 8.05am Southport to Preston service passes beneath Vicar's Bridge to enter Preston station. *Arnold Battson*

Right: Fairburn No 42675 with a Preston to Southport train approaches the ELR viaduct over the River Ribble. *Alan Castle*

Above: Penwortham Junction in 1962. *Arnold Battson*

Stanier Class 5 No 45200 crosses the ELR viaduct with the 3.04pm Preston to Southport service on 4 September 1964. *Peter Fitton*

Below: Stanier No 40197, heading a Preston to Southport train, is about to cross the ELR viaduct on 21 July 1956. *Ribble Steam Railway*

Below: Penwortham Junction is seen looking north on 2 March 1963, showing the original track on the left that led to the WLR Fishergate Hill station. *David Hampson*

'All stations to Southport'

Left: The bridge over Leyland Road, Penwortham, was known as the 'Cephos Bridge' – I wonder why! Note the gentleman reading his paper ill-advisedly stepping into the road! ('Cephos' was a cold and flu remedy from Cephos Ltd of Blackburn). *Lancashire Libraries*

Above: On 17 August 1964 a Fairburn tank works a local Southport to Preston service across Leyland Road. Note that the 'Cephos Bridge' has now assumed the name 'Jaguar Bridge'. *Alan Castle*

Penwortham Cop Lane

We now stop at the first station out of Preston, Penwortham Cop Lane, built by the L&YR in 1911, complete with two small booking offices/waiting rooms and 11 lamp posts – it never aspired to mains gas and electricity. Up to 1940 Penwortham Cop Lane station was simply called Cop Lane Halt. It was the only station on the line without any proper facilities for goods traffic.

Between Cop Lane and the next station, New Longton & Hutton, the train crosses over two level crossings at Back Lane and Lindle Lane, which are controlled by an endangered species, the level crossing keeper.

Penwortham Cop Lane station sign. *Alan Castle*

Above: Fairburn No 42158 pauses at Cop Lane with a Preston to Southport service on Sunday 16 August 1964. *Alan Castle*

Above: Tender-first No 78041 calls at Cop Lane with the 6.38pm Southport to Preston service on Wednesday 2 September 1964. *Alan Castle*

Above: Fairburn No 42286 leaves Cop Lane southbound, next stop New Longton & Sutton. *Alan Castl*

Left: Cop Lane station looking towards Hutton. *Alice Halliwell*

Above: A DMU at Cop Lane was a rarity on the branch where steam reigned supreme to the end. *Alan Castle*

'All stations to Southport'

The minor road crossing at Back Lane and the crossing keeper's domain, looking towards Cop Lane station. *Alan Castle*

Lindle Lane level crossing, with its wooden ground frame of 1900. *Tony Graham*

Left: Preston-bound 'Standard' No 78041 approaches Back Lane level crossing, between Cop Lane and New Longton & Hutton. *Alan Castle*

Right: Lindle Lane crossing, trackbed and crossing keeper's cottage are seen again following closure. *Graeme Heaton*

New Longton & Hutton and Longton Bridge

This station was still fairly busy in 1960 with commuters travelling in both directions, together with passengers using it for the nearby Lancashire Police Headquarters, Hutton Grammar School and the Agricultural College. Goods leaving the station included flowers, milk and veterinary products.

Longton Bridge station also served the village of Longton and was located next to a bridge crossing the A59.

Seen from the footplate of No 78041, a Southport to Preston service approaches New Longton & Hutton. *Alan Castle*

'All stations to Southport'

Above: Two views of New Longton & Hutton station in October 1963. In the first a solitary passenger awaits the next train, while the second thought-provoking scene features two mounted police officers proceeding over the level crossing. *Both Roger Roberts collection*

Left: In a tranquil scene on the branch, Riddles 2MT 2-6-0 No 78041 approaches New Longton & Hutton in the 1950s, while a shining Vauxhall Velox car provides a clue to the era. *Roger Roberts collection*

Right: On 23 August 1964 Ivatt Class 5 No 44686 is seen in a sylvan setting between Longton Bridge and New Longton & Hutton with the Saturdays-only 2.53pm Southport to Preston service. *David Hampson*

Stanier 2-6-4T No 42546 heads the 12.54pm Southport to Preston train at Longton Bridge on 2 March 1963. *Peter Fitton*

Bob Gregson

The Longton Bridge station buildings on the down platform.

Left: The up platform at Longton Bridge is seen on 2 September 1964, with Stanier 2-6-4T No 42645 arriving with a Southport-Preston service. *The late Frank Dean, Malcolm Richardson collection*

'All stations to Southport'

Above and below: Watch that smoke! Fowler No 42369 eases off the exhaust as it departs from Longton Bridge with the 2.16pm Southport to Preston service on Saturday 5 September 1964. It is a shame that none of this class have been preserved. *Both Alan Castle*

Hoole

Incredibly the remote Hoole station still had a full complement of staff, although the station master there also covered Longton Bridge. One versatile member of staff at Hoole had done it all – acting station master, porter, signalman, booking clerk – but it was soon to be the end of the era for proud station masters, porters and signalmen.

Right: In March 1960 the signalman opens the crossing gates at Hoole signal box, which adjoined the rural station. *Roger Roberts collection*

Left: Hoole signal box was an original Mackenzie & Holland type 3 design dating from 1882. *M. Mason*

Below: Looking towards Preston, Hoole station is complete with the usual branch-line fixtures. *John Williams*

Lament for a Branch Line

On 8 August 1964 the 12.37pm Saturdays-only service to Southport passes Hoole. *Tony Graham*

Stanier 2-6-4T No 42448 arrives at Hoole from Southport with the 12.40pm service to Preston on 8 August 1964. *David Hampson*

There are no passengers today at Hoole to greet Stanier Class 5 No 45078 on arrival with the 12.50pm service from Preston on 8 August 1964, only a month before complete closure. *David Hampson*

Hesketh Bank

On leaving the sleepy parish of Hoole, the view from the carriage window changes from suburbia to distinctly arable, with rich dark soil and open countryside dotted with market gardens and greenhouses all the way to Banks.

First we reach the River Douglas, which is crossed by a swing bridge to facilitate river navigation. On the south bank of the river the 1¼-mile Tarleton branch once veered off to reach the pier and boatyard where the paddle steamer *Virginia* once took Victorian tourists for a sail down the Ribble estuary to Lytham.

The familiar branch-line sound of clickety-clickety changes momentarily as the train crosses the river and passes over the points at Alty's brickworks on the approach to Hesketh Bank. This was perhaps the most important intermediate station on the branch, both for passengers and the despatch of local farm produce, as well as serving the local brickworks industry.

Reflections of the bridge over the River Douglas near Hesketh Bank, circa 1955. *Harry Mayor*

'All stations to Southport'

Left: A short distance beyond the River Douglas crossing was Alty's Hesketh Bank brickworks, with its own sidings. *John Ryan*

Below: Hesketh Bank's station sign. *Alan Castle*

Above: Hesketh Bank station, photographed in June 1954, was an important intermediate station on the branch, not only for the local brickworks but also for vegetable, freight and passenger traffic. *Gordon Biddle*

Left: Hesketh Bank station is seen on 29 August 1964, looking towards Preston shortly before closure of the branch. It is bereft of passengers – and note the derelict goods yard. *Roger Roberts collection*

Right: Fairburn 2-6-4T No 42158 is ready for departure from Hesketh Bank with a train to Preston on 2 September 1964. *The late Frank Dean, Malcolm Richardson collection*

No 78041 arrives at Hesketh Bank. *Ken Meek, Roger Roberts collection*

The period sign was big enough, so I guess there was no excuse for missing Hundred End! *Ribble Steam Railway*

Hundred End

A music hall joke arose from the next station along the line, Hundred End, which on account of the farming industry it served was known by the locals as 'Celery Junction'. When the porter chanted 'Hundred End' from the cinder platform of the loneliest outpost between Preston and Southport, you knew you had arrived – but where? It was like stepping back in time, to when generations of country folk who caught the trains here began to become aware that there might be life beyond the hamlet of Hundred End after all.

Hundred End station was justifiably yet another enigma, for its origins are obscure. Early Ordnance Survey maps published in 1878 and 1890 show it as Hundred End Gatehouse, by 1890 it has two short platforms, and in 1895 with wooden station buildings. Alongside the level crossing adjoining the two basic platforms was a fine timber-built L&YR signal box, dating from 1895. There were two crossovers and two goods sidings on the down (northbound) side.

For almost a century merchants had wheeled carts to these sidings and loaded produce into the wagons to begin railway journeys all over the country. The station buildings were all wooden and painted cherry red and cream, the traditional colours of the LMS. Oddly the booking office was detached from the platforms, situated on the opposite side of the road behind the signal box! And even there dimmed lighting was provided by modest oil lamps.

The somnolent rural station reminded me of the Will Hay and Moore Marriott film *Oh, Mr Porter!*, which conjured up a fanciful story about ghosts at Buggleskelly, a fictional country station. Amazingly Hundred End station still had a staff of three, but there was no sign of Will Hay! And unlike Buggleskelly the actual station master at Hundred End was real, and he also controlled Hesketh Bank and the next station along the line

'All stations to Southport'

A close-up of the booking office, signal box and level crossing at Hundred End. The box contained 19 levers and the gate wheel. This was a superb example of a Railway Signal Co box (with RSC decorative bargeboards). Supplied, as a single contract, to the WLR in 1895, two years before the L&YR takeover, the box survived until closure. *Ribble Steam Railway*

Hundred End station boasted this 'freight terminal' of yesteryear. The location was also known as 'Celery Junction' because of the amount of produce farmers sent to market from here. *Roger Roberts*

at Banks. The verse from the film also echoes the station's atmosphere and solitude: 'Every night when the moon is bright the miller's ghost is seen; the mill wheels turn though the night is still; he haunts the station he haunts the mill; and the line that lands in between.' At Hundred End the nearest windmill adjoined the huge late medieval freshwater marsh and lake known as Martin Mere.

On several occasions I recall being the only passenger to alight at Hundred End station, literally a lone 'wild west' outpost amidst endless rich agricultural fields, to go bird-watching on the remote Ribble marshes with my pal Harry Shorrock. We laughed at a colourful station poster promoting Weston-super-Mare at this unlikely rural outpost, which somehow seemed alien to travel expectations. Happy days – gone but not forgotten!

Banks

Banks station was often quite busy with passengers, as well as goods and local farm produce comprising potatoes, carrots, swedes, tomatoes, lettuce, beetroot and other vegetables, which were loaded into freight vans in the three-track goods yard. My friend the late Roger Roberts remembered his maiden great aunt Leah Wignall pushing a large hand cart through the streets of Banks to the station in the early hours on Saturday mornings, loaded with dressed chickens and vegetables to sell on her stall at Southport market. She remained with her cart in the guard's van for the 4-mile journey.

Above: Banks station, seen here looking towards Preston, was resplendent with signal box, level crossing, sidings and cattle pens and a small crane, all of which were typical of stations on the branch. *John Williams*

Above: At Banks station Stanier No 42435 is hauling the 10.00am service from Southport to Preston on 23 August 1964. *David Hampson*

Left: Stanier 2-6-4T No 42645 enters Banks with an up Preston train on 2 September 1964. *The late Frank Dean, Malcolm Richardson collection*

Right: Stanier 3MT 2-6-2T No 40197 arrives at Banks from Southport. *John Williams*

'All stations to Southport'

This LS&PJR viaduct at Blowick, with Butts Lane curve bridge, at Foul Lane in the far distance. *Roger Roberts*

Above right: On 8 August 1964 Fowler No 42369 is 'up front' on the 11.30am Preston to Southport service near Crossens. *David Hampson*

Right: Crossens station was the terminus of the electric trains than ran from Liverpool to Southport and on to Crossens, which began on 22 March 1904. *Bob Gregson*

Crossens

We re-enter suburbia at Crossens, where the green electric multiple units terminate. The L&YR introduced electrification between Liverpool, Southport and Crossens on 22 March 1904, and the company held the distinction of running the longest non-stop electric train during trials between Crossens and Liverpool on 6 March of that year. The system operated on the third-rail system at 600V dc.

Churchtown

Between Crossens and Hesketh Park the track was steeply graded on either side of the intermediate station of Churchtown. The station's wooden platform was above the road, and here passengers in the commuter belt boarded and alighted from both steam-hauled and electric trains. From here consignments of locally caught fish were once loaded onto trains for despatch all over the country.

Above: Stanier Class 5 No 44940 heads the 9.30am Southport to Preston service at Churchtown on 23 August 1964. *David Hampson*

Above right: On Sunday 30 August 1964 No 42158 hauls the 9.24am Southport to Preston service past Churchtown. *Keith Hick*

Right: At Churchtown the station platforms were elevated high above street level and constructed entirely of wood. *Alan Castle*

'All stations to Southport'

Above: Fairburn 2-6-4T No 42675 enters Churchtown with the 12.27pm Preston to Southport train on 11 August 1964. *Chris Spring*

Above right: Class 5 No 44818 arrives at Churchtown from Preston with a Southport train on 4 September 1964. *Roger Roberts*

Left: 'Jubilee' No 45715 *Invincible* worked the 6.24pm Preston to Southport service on 28 August 1962, and is seen here near Churchtown. *Ribble Steam Railway*

Right: Stanier Class 5 No 44940 departing Churchtown with the 9.30am Southport to Preston service on 23 August 1964. *David Hampson*

Hesketh Park

This station served a residential area alongside Southport's Hesketh Park. It was well kept, and the winner of prizes in the Best Kept Garden competition, and had a characteristic small signal box at the end of the platform. The station was named after the nearby Hesketh Park, which had been laid out on land that was historically covered by sand dunes.

Left: The exterior of Hesketh Park station from the approach road.

Below left: Just one and a half passengers await the 3.22pm service from Hesketh Park to Southport on 1 August 1964.
Roger Roberts

Above: Class 5 No 45375 arrives at Hesketh Park station with the 10.30am Preston to Southport service on 8 August 1964.
David Hampson

Right: Stanier tank No 42476 approaches Hesketh Park with a down Preston to Southport train on 3 August 1956.
Ribble Steam Railway

'All stations to Southport'

St Luke's

Steam trains on the Preston to Southport branch avoided Meols Cop by taking the avoiding line to the west of the station. On the final approach to Southport was St Luke's station (now demolished), which was of timber construction.

Right and below: The exterior St Luke's and a general view of the station in September 1968. *Both Jim Peden*

Above: A picturesque lattice footbridge near Hesketh Park. *R. C. Chown, Roger Roberts collection*

Bob Gregson

Right: Stanier Class 5 No 45337 hauls the 9.43am Preston to Southport service at St Luke's on 8 August 1964. *David Hampson*

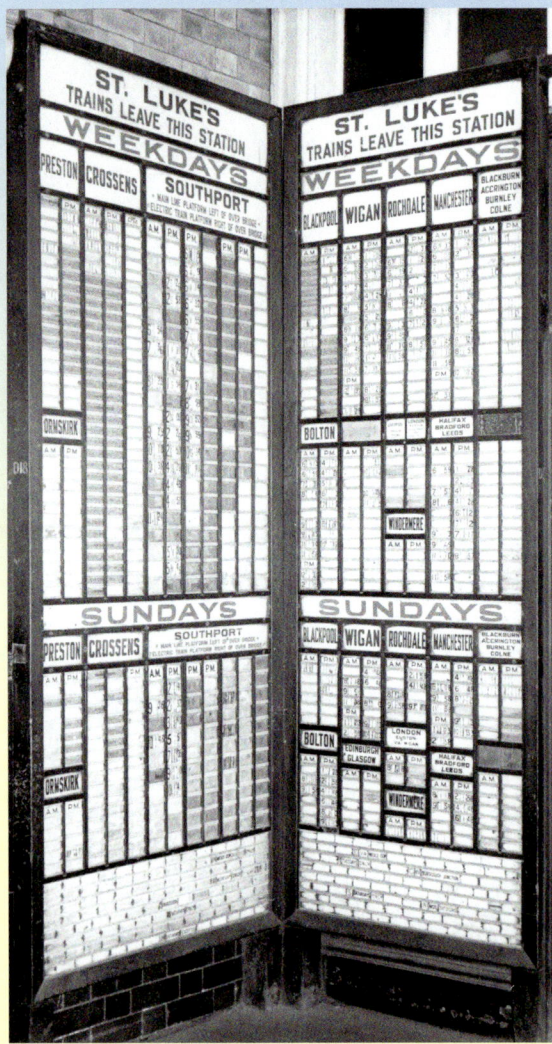

Left: The attractive departure board at St Luke's, photographed in September 1968. *Jim Peden, B. G. Barlow collection*

Southport Chapel Street

On the approach to Southport an opportunity arises for an impromptu bout of trainspotting, as our train passes the engine sheds. In 1961 St Luke's and Chapel Street stations were the haunt of the last surviving ex-L&YR Aspinall Class 2P 'Radial' 2-4-2T, No 50850 (formerly numbered 675). I managed to see this old-timer from the carriage window in the early 1960s before arriving at Southport and the end of the line. Unfortunately it was the end of line too for No 50850, built at the L&YR's Horwich Works, where the entire class of more than 100 had been constructed. It would have been well worthy of preservation had it not gained a one-way ticket to Crewe to be scrapped.

Signalling at Chapel Street was a mixture of upper-

Left: L&YR pneumatic signals at Southport Chapel Street. The signal box was above the station approach tracks and not of the more familiar design. *Jim Peden*

Left: A light freight train leaves the Southport marshalling yards powered by Stanier Class 5 No 44767 on 8 February 1964. *Arnold Battson*

Right: On 3 May 1964 Southport's own 'Patriot', No 45527 *Southport*, was on shed at Blackpool. *Roger Roberts*

Below: Ex-L&YR 2-4-2T No 50850 is assigned to shunting in the carriage sidings at Southport on 1 October 1959. *Roger Roberts collection*

quadrant semaphores and more recently installed colour-light signals. The semaphore signals and lights were operated by an electro-pneumatic system that came into use at Southport stion box on 4 November 1917, St Lukes box on 23 June 1918, with the main line being quadrupled from Southport station to St Lukes on 15 June 1919.

At its peak, Chapel Street station had 11 regular platforms and two excursion platforms. Today only six truncated platforms are in use (Platforms 1-3 for Liverpool trains and 4-6 for Manchester). The Crossens EMU service used Platform 9 & 10. Platforms 7 to 10 have been demolished and the land is now a car park. Most of the present station building is a shopping centre and the station's glory days as a holiday destination are long gone, as we will see in the next chapter.

Above left: In this panoramic view of Chapel Street station, No 78041 departs with the 1.17pm service for Preston on the day the line closed for good. *Alan Castle*

Above right: Stanier 3MT 2-6-2T tank No 40195 waits with a Preston-bound train in October 1956. *Ribble Steam Railway*

Left and right and opposite: Exterior and interior period views of Southport Chapel Street. *All Arnold Battson*

'All stations to Southport'

Historically the Southport to Preston branch continued largely in its L&YR form. Its stations and signal boxes had maintained a link with the past, and survived into British Railways days through to closure.

Right: 'Ten Bristol tipped, box of Swan matches, packet of Opal Fruits and tube of Polo mints, please.' *Roger Roberts*

Right: W. H. Smith kiosks were very much a feature of railway stations in the days of steam. *Roger Roberts*

Left: Stanier tank No 42634 waits at the now demolished Platform 9 with a Preston-bound train in 1964. *Jim Peden*

Below left: Stanier tank No 42435 waits at Southport ready to take on water on 4 September 1964. *Peter Fitton*

Right: Class 5 No 45156 is ready to depart from Chapel Street in May 1966. This particular engine was named *Ayrshire Yeomanry*. *Arnold Battson*

Centre right: Stanier tank No 42645 is about to depart from Chapel Street with the 1.50pm service to Preston on 27 July 1963. *David Hampson*

Below: BR 'Standard' No 75017 is ready to depart from Southport on 15 July 1960. *Roger Carpenter*

8 • The heyday of the Preston to Southport branch

The railways revolutionised travel and have played an important part of the history of our country for more than two centuries. During the mid to late 19th century the established railway network fundamentally changed the dynamic forces of Britain for ever.

At the time of the building of the West Lancashire Railway in 1882, Southport was served by three separate railway termini and was even more popular than Blackpool, prior to a link being established with the Preston & Wyre Railway at Poulton-le-Fylde in 1846 to a new station at Blackpool North.

Unlike Blackpool's reliance on the railway, Southport was already established as a holiday resort by 1820, with visitors arriving by canal boats and horse-drawn carriages. The 1840s were by far the biggest decade for railway growth and from the start they were used for excursion traffic. The underlying principle of the excursion train was that trains conveyed passengers to and from a variety of predetermined venues, with the benefits of travelling at reduced rates. Probably the first organised railway excursion took place on 5 July 1841 when 32-year-old Thomas Cook engaged an excursion train to carry about 500 temperance supporters from Leicester to a meeting in Loughborough. Railway excursions ushered in the mass market for leisure, with thousands of passengers taking advantage of the reduced fares to popular seaside resorts in Lancashire and throughout the country.

Through the connection of the Southport branch with the L&YR station at Preston, which opened in July 1900, an important holiday trade began with the towns and cities of Scotland and northern England. The terminus of the East Lancashire's line from Manchester was originally at London Street station which closed on 1 April 1857 and lay derelict until 1873 when it was converted into a carriage repair shop. It was closed on 23 December 1912 and replaced by Meols Cop repair shops Demolition of London Street repair shop and London Street goods shed took place in 1913, platforms 7 to 11 at Chapel Street were built over the site of the repair shops, the excursion platforms were built over the site of London Street goods shed and sidings, replacing a smaller excursion platform of 1876 which had been slightly nearer St Lukes.

The summer excursion traffic over the Preston to Southport branch was closely associated with Wakes Weeks, which were a legacy of the Industrial Revolution. In northern England the Wakes were originally governed by the resilient textile industry; many workers simply refused to turn in after a brief holiday, so mill-owners closed factories to clean and service machines while thousands of employees enjoyed their annual holiday. Nowadays the Wakes are in permanent slumber, and the weaving sheds of Lancashire and Yorkshire are silent with not a single bobbin left turning.

In the Midlands at Burton-on-Trent the Bass Brewery began to offer its employees and their families a day out to the seaside by excursion trains. By 1889 this had become a regular event with as many as 15 trains leaving Burton en route to the coast with up to 10,000 people in eager anticipation of their arrival. Imagine the logistical management involved! Sometimes there were as many as 10 separate trains setting off at the same time. This phenomenon was repeated throughout Lancashire, bringing steam-hauled trains into Southport Chapel Street and Blackpool Central.

The British railway poster came of age in 1923 at the time of the Grouping of the railway companies. Each company advertised its routes through posters and brochures, with the emphasis on seaside resorts and places rich in scenic grandeur and heritage, as well as resorts and cities offering a range of cultural interests. Leading poster artists were employed to persuade passengers to travel by train. In 1924 the famous Southport Flower Show began and had become the largest in the world by the outbreak of the Second World War, with correspondingly heavy excursion traffic into the resort.

The heyday of the Preston to Southport branch closely paralleled the 'Wakes' from the 1920s up to the beginning of the 'Swinging Sixties'. The

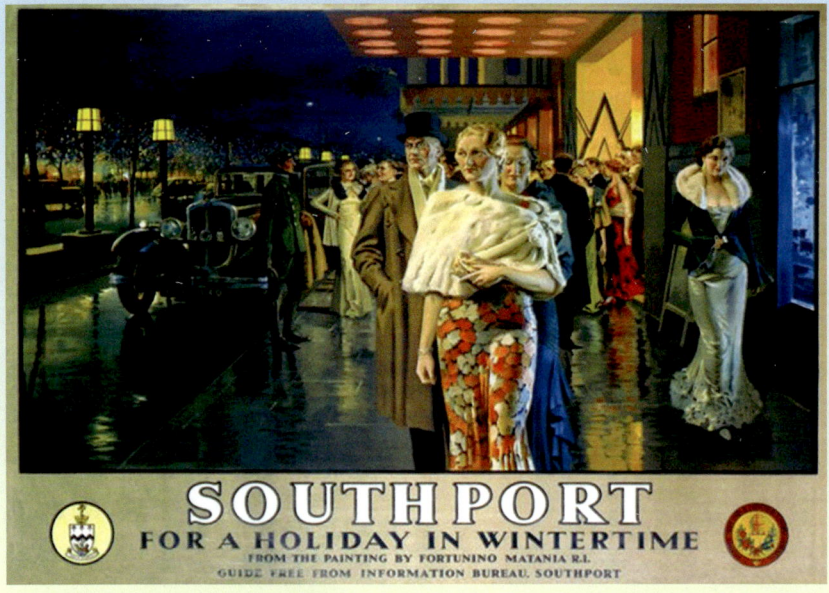

Above and above right: Railway companies promoted Southport through their colourful posters, attracting the public to the resort from all over the country.
Bob Gregson

Left: An LMS advertisement for 'Sunny Southport' to see the Southport Flower Show, which has long been an attraction.

Right: 'B1' No 61050 is on foreign tracks at Southport with a Flower Show special excursion in August 1963.
Jim Peden, B. G. Barlow collection

The heyday of the Preston to Southport branch

Above: Excursion trains wait to depart from Chapel Street on 14 June 1963.
The late Frank Dean, Malcolm Richardson collection

Above right: Hughes Fowler 'Crab' 2-6-0 No 42860 is lined up against rakes of passenger carriages at Chapel Street's excursion platforms on 14 June 1963. *The late Frank Dean, Malcolm Richardson collection*

Left and right: Aspinall 2-4-2T No 50781 works at Southport Chapel Street at the height of the holiday season on 31 August 1959. The MPD is on the right of the first view. *Both Peter Fitton*

LMS timetable of May 1939 shows how busy the branch had become, with 26 trains a day each way and eight on Sunday. There were diagrammed through trains to and from Glasgow, Yorkshire, Accrington, Colne, Todmorden, Morecambe and Newcastle (via Tebay).

By the 1950s, and the gradual slowing down of the 'Wakes Weeks', there were still 20 trains a day each way between Preston and Southport and six on Sunday. The BR London Midland Region timetable for that period also advertised through workings between Southport and Accrington, Padiham, Burnley and Todmorden. During the summer holidays of the early 1960s day excursions and mystery rail trips to and from seaside resorts like Southport were also popular. Holidaymakers from Glasgow thronged the resort's boarding houses and day trippers took advantage of excursions visiting the resort. Just 'imagine' – a 'day tripper' with a cheap day return 'ticket to ride'

Left: An unidentified Aspinall 2P 2-4-2T departs from Chapel Street with five carriages on excursion passenger train duty on 25 June 1938. *E. R. Morten*

Far left: Glamour girls on Southport sands in the 1930s. *Bob Gregson*

Below: Stanier 2-6-4T No 42662 powers the Saturdays-only Glasgow to Southport holiday service through Longton Bridge on 23 August 1964. *David Hampson*

The heyday of the Preston to Southport branch

Left: 'Caprotti' Class 5 No 44745 enters New Longton & Hutton with the Summer only 10.00am SX Southport to Blackpool Central arriving at 11.00am on 11 August 1964.
Chris Spring

Right: Stanier No 42537 leaves Hesketh Park with the 8.00am Southport to Accrington service arriving at 9.05am on 27 March 1957; this train served holidaymakers employed in the textile industry in Lancashire and Yorkshire.
Arnold Battson

Left: BR 'Standard' Class 4MT 4-6-0 No 75017 departs from Chapel Street for Todmorden on the 14 June 1963. The extended London Street excursion platforms are top right. *The late Frank Dean, Malcolm Richardson collection*

Below: Stanier 2-6-4T No 42546 powers the 9.48am Accrington to Southport service at Cherry Tree, carrying more day trippers and holidaymakers to the resort on 25 May 1963. *Peter Fitton*

Left: Fairburn No 42061 passes St Luke's with an excursion to Glasgow. *Jim Peden, B. G. Barlow collection*

Right: Stanier 8F No 48202 switches from its usual freight to passenger duties with an excursion train passing St Luke's on 15 July 1962. *Jim Peden, B. G. Barlow collection*

Below left: 'B1' No 61337 brings an excursion into Southport from the North East on 18 May 1964. *Jim Peden, B. G. Barlow collection*

Below: 'Royal Scot' Class No 46133 *The Green Howards* passes St Luke's on the approach to Southport circa 1960. *Jim Peden, B. G. Barlow collection*

The heyday of the Preston to Southport branch

from Preston to Southport could have caught up with the Beatles, who travelled Lancashire and Merseyside extensively from 1961 to late 1964; they appeared at the Kingsway Club, Southport, as well as the Odeon Cinema about 12 times between March 1961 and October 1963.

By a strange irony, the number of passengers arriving at Southport during August 1964 was 504,973, an increase of 126,749 on the same month in 1963. However, there were no grounds for optimism regarding the closure of the Preston to Southport branch line, scheduled for 6 September

Right: A British Railways flyer for 12 June to 10 September 1961 inclusive showed that up to 20 excursion trains were departing from Southport Chapel Street to the same number of destinations every day.

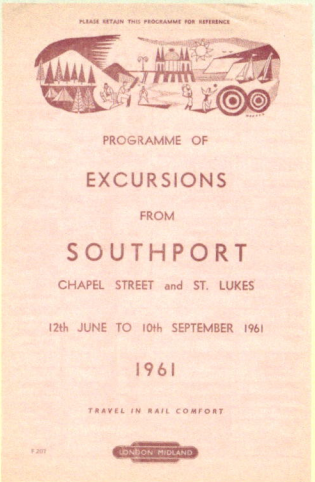

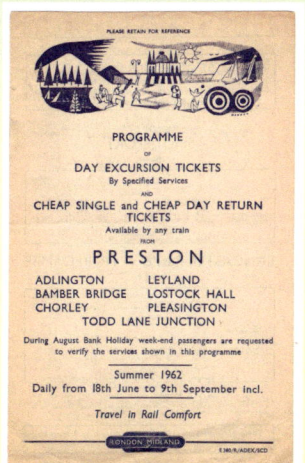

Above left: BR 'Standard' Class 4 No 75033 powers a long train through St Luke's full of passengers who just want to enjoy being 'beside the seaside'. *Jim Peden, B. G. Barlow collection*

Above: Stanier tank No 42445 passes under the A59 (Longton Bypass bridge) at New Longton on a Southport to Preston service on 2 September 1964, marking the twilight of Southport as a holiday resort, and of the branch. *Ribble Steam Railway*

Left: During the summer of 1962 a programme of extra day return excursions ran from various stations via Preston to Southport.

Left: With more carriages than the usual three, the 9.43am service from Preston to Southport, hauled by Fairburn No 42061, stops at Banks station on 23 August 1964 *David Hampson*

Above: Riddles BR 'Standard No 78022 runs through pleasant countryside near New Longton with a typical Preston to Southport train on 23 August 1964. *David Hampson*

Above left and right: The Holiday Runabout Tickets (Area 2 covered Southport) cost £1 2s 6d for six days and was good value, leading to day trippers flocking to Southport from Preston and further afield. *Roger Roberts collection*

The heyday of the Preston to Southport branch

1964, despite the lovely hot summer weather coinciding with Southport Flower Show.

I look back on happy train rides from Preston to Southport with my parents in the late 1950s. On arrival there was the opportunity to visit the pleasure ground and take a ride on the big dipper at the resort's Pleasureland, or go out to sea in an ex-wartime amphibious craft that saw action during the 'D' Day landings. Taking a daring flight on a small aircraft that took off and landed on the sands was a whole new experience, and definitely not for the faint-hearted! On Southport Pier could be found the now closed Pier Tramway, which was more than 3,600 feet (1,100m) long and conveyed passengers from the promenade to the pier head.

The Lakeside Miniature Railway still passes under the pier, carrying passengers alongside the marine lake between the town centre and the sea. Its claim to fame is that it is said to be the oldest continuously running 15-inch-gauge (381mm) railway in the world. Town centre attractions included the famous Lord Street, an elegant Victorian tree-lined shopping street with a host of art deco cinemas on the south side, while the magnificent edifice of the former Lord Street station stood proud across the street.

During the 1950s the seaside entertainment industry continued to entertain holidaymakers with veterans of the music hall stage playing the Garrick Theatre next to Lord Street station. This theatre was built on the site of the Southport Opera House, part of the complex of the Southport Winter Gardens, which opened on 7 September 1891 but was destroyed by fire in 1929. Throughout its 25-year life as a variety theatre, the Garrick presented summer variety shows, musical comedies, drama and pantomime

Unfortunately, there was nothing to sustain either the ailing fortunes of the Garrick Theatre, which saw its final curtain in 1957, or for that matter the Preston to Southport branch line, and a tentative parallel may be drawn. A combination of changing tastes, including established television in 1953, increasing car ownership and a brand-new era of package holidays to Mediterranean resorts displaced the Lancashire seaside resorts as holiday destinations, and thousands of theatres, branch lines and stations closed throughout Britain in the 1960s, including the Preston to Southport line.

The British Railways summer timetable for 1964 shows the reduced service of steam trains between Southport Chapel Street and Preston, with the first of 15 weekday trains departing from Southport at 5.47am and the last arriving at Preston at 11.58pm. Only six trains ran on Sundays. In addition to the steam service, 34 electric trains ran from Southport to Crossens and return, with no Sunday running. The EMU service was contained within the urban sprawl of Southport and catered for commuters, in contrast to the rural character of the stations beyond, which were served by steam-hauled services.

By 1964 the seaside resort of Southport and this rural branch line that served it were about to hit the buffers for good. Quite clearly the writing was on the wall for the branch and for the golden age of the once popular adage, 'Oh, I do like to be beside the seaside'.

Southport holidaymakers and the jam-packed Lakeside Miniature Railway circa 1950. *Roger Roberts collection*

Southport's Lakeside Miniature Railway. *Bob Gregson*

The BR 1964 summer timetable.

9 • Modernisation: the beginning of the end

In post-war Britain the railway network was run down and, unlike railways on the continent, there was still a large dependence on steam traction. As a young lad, while trainspotting in the early-to-mid-1950s at Preston station I was fortunate to witness the glory days of steam locomotives, at a time when they were still being manufactured. These included the continuation of existing designs of the 'Big Four' to replace tired and worn-out locomotives, supplemented by a new range of standard designs to be used across the British Railways network.

Between 1948 and 1960 British Railways built 2,537 steam locomotives. They were destined to lead short lives, some as little as five years against a design life of more than 30. They included Riddles 2MT 2-6-0 No 78041, which hauled the last passenger train before closure of the branch. British Railways steam locomotives working the branch were mainly shedded at Lostock Hall and Derby Road Motive Power Depots.

The Modernisation Plan of 1955 was intended to bring British Railways up to date and included the gradual withdrawal of steam and the phasing in of diesel traction. The replacement programme marked a sudden change in policy by BR, which until 1955 had continued to favour steam traction. A Government White Paper produced in 1956 stated that modernisation would help to eliminate British Railways' financial deficit by 1962. The goal was to increase speed, reliability, safety and line capacity through a series of measures that would make services more attractive to passengers and freight operators, thereby recovering traffic that was being lost to the new road network, at a time when the first motorway in the country – the Preston Bypass (M6) – opened in 1957.

The Modernisation Plan called for the rapid and large-scale introduction of diesel locomotives – a total of 2,500

Top right: Type 4 (later Class 40) No 338 waits in the excursion platforms at Southport on 22 July 1965. Modernisation was well under way in that year, but not for the Preston to Southport branch, which had by now closed. *Jim Peden, B. G. Barlow collection*

Right: A diverted Preston to Liverpool DMU is seen at Roe Lane Junction on 3 March 1963. *Arnold Battson*

– which were to be acquired in 10 years at a cost of £345 million. This meant that many steam locomotives were scrapped when only a few years old and often before a reliable and practical diesel or electric equivalent was available. Consequently in some instances the newly introduced diesels broke down and were towed away by the surviving steam locomotives they were meant to replace. The sudden introduction of prototype diesel locomotives and the first batch of diesel multiple units was ongoing during the early 1960s. The appropriately named Class 9F 2-10-0 No 92220 *Evening Star* was the last steam locomotive to be built by British Railways, in 1960, heralding the beginning of the end for steam on British Railways.

On 27 March 1963 Dr Richard Beeching published his first report, *The Reshaping of British Railways*, Part 1. Sadly his plan to 'reshape' the railways led to the unprecedented contraction of the national railway network. The report listed the Preston to Southport line and its nine intermediate stations from Hesketh Park to Penwortham Cop Lane for closure, included within the national total of 5,000 miles of track and 2,263 stations and halts. This modernisation programme led to vast inroads into the massive fleet of the various classes of splendid steam engines of all shapes and sizes, both nationally and locally. At the beginning of 1968 there were still approximately 350 steam engines at work in North West England, but a rapid succession of withdrawals led to the grand finale of steam in regular service on 4 August 1968. Inevitably this heralded the closure of the last three remaining engine sheds on the BR network and the scrapping of thousands of steam locomotives.

Preston's Lostock Hall shed sidings became a morgue for row upon row of locomotives with their chimneys draped by an ominous sack prior to a final journey to the breaker's yard.

The Southport branch had always served thinly populated rural districts and was an obvious candidate for the infamous Beeching 'axe'. Moreover, Hundred End station in particular had

Left: The announcement of the closure to all traffic of Hundred End in 1962. *Arnold Battson*

Below: The lost world of Hundred End: Stanier Class 5 No 44745 passes through the by now closed station with a Southport to Preston service on 23 August 1964. *David Hampson*

undeniably justified closure; the reality was that the daily takings at the booking office averaged only £1 with a grand total of ten passengers a day in 1961. The station had already closed to goods in 1960 and was the first along the branch to close to passengers, on 30 April 1962, foreshadowing complete closure of the branch line two years later.

Following publication of the Beeching Report the end of the line came very quickly following the statutory procedures and adherence to caveats. On 21 May 1964 the *Southport Visiter*'s lead story read:

'The Minister of Transport has agreed to the withdrawal of the railway passenger train service between Southport and Preston.

Modernisation: the beginning of the end

Looking in the opposite direction on the same day, Stanier 2-6-4T No 42435 passes through Hundred End with the 12.37pm Preston to Southport service. *David Hampson*

The site of Hundred End station is now occupied by a bungalow. *Mark Bartlett*

Withdrawal is subject to the revision of certain existing bus services. Nine stations will be closed and the Southport to Crossens electric service will be discontinued. The date on which the closure will be implemented has yet to be decided, but will be announced when the conditions imposed by the Minister have been met.'

A public enquiry was held at the Cambridge Hall, Southport, on 19 October 1963, when figures produced showed a revenue of £52,700 against running costs of £175,600 for 1962. These figures were taken from a memorandum issued in August 1963 by the London Midland Region of the British Railways Board at Manchester to the Chairman and members of the North West Area Transport Users Consultative Committee. The memorandum stated that 'the total population serviced by the line, excluding the towns of Southport and Preston, was approximately 27,590 and apart from some light industry at Crossens the remainder of the area served by the railway is mainly devoted to agriculture and market gardening.' Reference was made to alternative rail routes available and the comparable cost and frequency of bus services, which were to be improved. An estimated extra expenditure of £35,746 was needed if the line was to be left open for five years for permanent way, signalling, bridges and building maintenance.

A survey yielded that on a daily average 724 passengers alighted from a total of 34 trains on Saturdays and 679 on weekdays on the Crossens to Southport electric service. On the line to Preston as few as two or three passengers boarded some early-morning trains from Southport, and on only one train, the 4.14pm from Southport on Saturday, did the average rise to more than 100. Apart from light industry at Crossens, the service covered an agricultural and market gardening area. Excluding Preston and Southport, the total population of villages amounted to 27,950, though the figure was expected to rise to 43,000 within 20 years. The growth would be centred mainly on Penwortham, where better road passenger services were planned;

the alternative rail route from Southport to East Lancashire would still be available through Wigan.

Among the objectors was the Secretary of the local Hotel & Guest House Association, who stated:

'It is vitally important that excursion trains from Scotland, Yorkshire and the far north are not withdrawn. We have been assured that these trains will be diverted via Wigan and Burscough. Southport is becoming more popular with Scottish families and we want to see special trains operating from Glasgow Fair Week and throughout the season.'

In conclusion, it was clear from the beginning that the West Lancashire Railway would never be a viable entity. Notwithstanding the financial problems that beset the railway, the tenacity and ingenuity of those early promoters and officials had made the line a reality and they, and those who followed them, kept the trains running for 86 years. The line had always been used for the conveyance of some freight as well as the conveyance of schoolchildren and tourism, and all-encompassing business travel in the broadest sense of the word. It would be sadly missed, but harsh economics had overruled sentiment.

That the line could not have survived after the Beeching Report of 1962 was never in any doubt. Alas, the glory days of Britain's regional branch lines as part of the railway network are long gone. Like so many others at that time, the West Lancashire Railway was to pass into history almost unnoticed. With passengers rarely exceeding 100 it is not surprising that the infamous 'axe' was to be swung, with the execution planned for Sunday 6 September 1964, and the subject of the next chapter.

On Saturday 5 September 1964, the day before closure of the branch, this was the view from Vicar's Bridge of the Preston terminus of the Southport branch, featuring 'Jubilee' No 45715 *Invincible* and Stanier No 42547 on a Southport-bound train. *Peter Fitton*

Suitably daubed with the infamous Beeching 'axe', No 76081 is ready to depart from Southport at 9.30pm on Saturday 5 September 1964 with the last through service to Accrington. *Alan Castle*

10 • A night to remember: 6 September 1964

With no late stay of execution, which was planned for Sunday 6 September 1964, Mr F. Winters, the station master at Southport Chapel Street, is reported to have said: 'People from far and wide will come to Southport on Sunday evening for the last trip to Preston before the passenger service closes and the line fades into history, including many members of the Railway Correspondence & Travel Society.'

British Railways foresaw a good attendance of nostalgia-seeking passengers and put on three extra carriages to make a total of six. Preston station was crowded with hundreds of people waiting for BR 'Standard' 2-6-0 No 78041 to depart from the East Lancashire platform. The last steam-hauled service train to run from Preston to Southport left Preston at 10.35pm and arrived at Southport Chapel Street at 11.10pm, 10 minutes late. The last steam-hauled service passenger train from Southport to Preston departed at 10.20pm and was hauled by Fairburn tank No 42296, with 220 passengers on board.

The two trains left on time and at each station there were onlookers waiting in eager anticipation to greet them, with cars sounding their horns at level crossings to say goodbye. The two trains passed at Hesketh Bank, where more than 300 people gathered on the platform, including the Hesketh Bank Silver Band, to give the trains a rousing musical send-off. After passing Cop Lane, exploding detonators rounded off the journey in the same way that the birth of the WLR had been celebrated 82 years earlier, but this time it was symbolic of a funeral. Into the darkness they went for the very last time, recalling a bygone railway age that had existed since the late Victorian era.

Railway photographers lined the route throughout the day with cameras at the ready, producing for posterity a fine portfolio of photographs of the last trains. The locomotives hauling the last trains were appropriately adorned with headboards bearing the words '1882-1964 Last Day'. The last electric train had run from Southport to Crossens the preceding evening, Saturday 5 September. The 'axe' had been wielded, and Nos 42296 and 78041 would soon be visiting the scrapyard.

The *Lancashire Evening Post* carried the headline 'Crowds cheer the Scrapyard Special', and the following account:

'It was said to be a funeral but instead it turned out to be a wild party with singing, chanting, laughter, good humour, fireworks and the odd tear. This was the night that the Preston to Southport line died as it had never lived, with practically every carriage full. Sunday 6th September 1964 will go down as a night to remember; a night when we British showed what a sentimental lot we are; a night when over 100 passenger sang Auld Lang Syne as the train rumbled into the stations; a night when all along the line people waved and cheered.

It all began shortly after 10 o'clock at Southport, when a sad voice crackled over the microphone, "The last train to Preston will shortly depart from Platform 9. This is a sad occasion as tomorrow the line closes. We thank you for your past support."

With that hordes of train enthusiasts scrambled into their compartments. With the hands of the clock pointing at 10.20pm, history was made when the guard, Ron Gillibrand of Preston, waved his green lamp. With a hiss and a clatter No 42296 pulled away with a blast on its whistle, with 220 on board.'

Following closure of the line, first to go was most of the track and the crucial bridges over watercourses, including that over the River Douglas. The track was lifted during 1965, including the goods-only line to Fishergate Hill station in Preston. The trackbed was gradually sold off piecemeal to farmers and developers. A freight service to a coal siding at Hesketh Park continued until November 1967, then the remaining track was lifted in late 1968. However, a small stump remained in place as far as Roe Lane in Southport until the very early 1970s as part of the Meols Cop Electric Depot complex.

Above: No 78041 departs from Preston with the 10.12am Preston to Southport service on the last day, Sunday 6 September 1964, with just a few more journeys to do before it reached the ultimate end of the line. All the following photographs were taken on that day. *Alan Castle*

Above centre: The same locomotive is seen at Preston later with the 1.16pm train from Southport. *Alan Castle*

Right: No 78041 passes Southport signal box with the 1.17pm service to Preston. *John Williams*

Above far right: Fowler 2-6-4T No 42369 negotiates the curve from Whitehouse West with a Southport to Preston service. *Luke Kay*

Longton & Hutton level crossing and signal box, view looking north. *John Williams*

The wooden waiting room on the down platform at Penwortham Cop Lane, with clock, seat and oil lamp. *Both John Williams*

No 78041 calls at Cop Lane with the 2.34pm service from Preston. *John Williams*

A friend of the late Alan Castle prepared the special commemorative headboard for No 78041, seen to good effect as it departs from Platform No 8 at Southport with the 1.17pm train to Preston on 6 September 1964. *Ribble Steam Railway*

A night to remember: 6 September 1964

No 78041 calls at Hesketh Bank. *John Williams*

An L&YR bridge notice at Hesketh Bank. *John Williams*

Hoole station buildings on the down platform. *John Williams*

This is Longton Bridge station looking towards Preston; the upper quadrant signal in the 'off' position for the last time. *John Williams*

Above: A close-up of No 78041 at Crossens – there's no doubting the sad occasion. *John Williams*

Above right: Crossens station and footbridge, looking towards Preston. *John Williams*

Right: Banks station and signal box, looking towards Preston. *John Williams*

Far right: Hundred End station is already closed, but the signal box is still in business on the last day. *John Williams*

A night to remember: 6 September 1964

The following sequence of pictures along the line from Southport to Preston was taken on the last day of operations. *Below:* This is Hesketh Park station looking towards Preston, viewed from under the footbridge. *John Williams*

Churchtown station is viewed looking towards Preston, with arriving Fairburn tank No 42289. *John Williams*

No 78041, working the 6.52pm service from Preston, enters Crossens station. *John Williams*

Above: The distinctive Hesketh Park signal box, 1878-1968. *John Williams*

A night to remember: 6 September 1964

Fixing the last day headboard to No 78041. *Bob Gregson*

A final scramble for the very last train from Preston to Southport?? From today consensus itself will be consigned to the last chance saloon. *Roger Roberts collection*

Above: At Chapel Street station No 42296 waits to depart. *Alan Castle*

Above right: Driver and fireman reflect on the end of an era at Preston station. *Alan Castle*

Right: It's goodnight to Cop Lane station and the Southport branch. *Alan Castle*

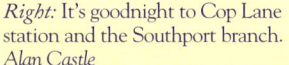

11 • Not au revoir but goodbye to the Preston to Southport branch

Despite any suggestions to the contrary, I am confident that this particular branch can never be reinstated – hundreds of dwellings and land reclamation have guaranteed that. Much of the trackbed has been reclaimed for agricultural use, all significant bridges demolished and the Penwortham bypass replacing rail. Network Rail now runs all Wigan and Manchester trains via Meols Cop station, which survives, and they pass the site of the now demolished St Luke's station. However, restoring curves to the north of Burscough would link the Preston to Ormskirk line with the Wigan to Southport line; the cost would be relatively small and once again Preston would have a rail link with Southport.

Nothing much is left to see of the old WLR nearly 60 years after closure, with only overgrown embankments, a few scars on the landscape and isolated stone bridge abutments standing as testament to the erstwhile railway.

The site of Hesketh Bank station is now a housing estate and the road bridge alongside has been levelled, leaving no evidence that a railway or station ever existed. However, the West Lancashire Light Railway rekindles the age of steam and serves as a poignant reminder of the branch, operating as a heritage narrow-gauge steam railway on the site of Hesketh Bank brickworks. It is close to the original WLR and the company aims to extend its line onto part of the former WLR trackbed. The working museum was founded in 1967 and is now home to a remarkable collection of six historic narrow-gauge steam, petrol, diesel and electric locomotives. The line is open to the public from April to November and trains operate on Sundays and Bank Holidays along a short line around the old clay pit – telephone 01772 815881 for further information.

The ELR viaduct at Preston and the trackbed, which now leads to the Preston Junction Nature Reserve, survive as a cycleway and footpath. The Whitehouse triangle is still discernible with the two links to the ELR track, and the trackbed under the bridge carrying the West Coast Main Line is walkable. The piers of the old railway bridge that once spanned the Ribble alongside Penwortham old bridge close to the original Fishergate Hill station also remain as a legacy of the original course of the railway that once ran from Preston to Southport.

Burscough Bridge Junction, looking east on 28 August 1979, with the southern curve heading right towards Ormskirk. *R. B. Blenkowe*

Not au revoir but goodbye to the Preston to Southport branch

Who said anything about the last train – or should I say last permanent way vehicle? It is being propelled by Alan Castle near Longton Bridge.

A goods train at Hesketh Park is hauled by Class 5 No 45055 on 1 July 1965, by which time the track had been singled. *Jim Peden, B. G. Barlow collection*

Hesketh Park signal box (L&YR No 601 of 1878) March 1968. *Tony Graham*

9F 2-10-0 No 92053 is engaged in track-lifting at Churchtown. *Keith Hick*

Track removal in 1965 at Whitehouse West, looking towards Middleforth Junction. *Luke Kay*

Above: Stanier 2-6-4T No 42645 heads a Preston to Southport train off the curve at Whitehouse West Junction on 4 September 1964. The second picture shows the same location with the permanent way permanently removed in 1965. *Both Luke Kay*

Above: The site of Whitehouse North signal box looking towards Todd Lane in July 1987. *Luke Kay*

Below: Whitehouse North Junction, looking towards Preston in 1965 with the Southport track removed. *Luke Kay*

Below and right: A Type 4 diesel on the WCML passes over the Preston to Southport branch at Whitehouse West. The second view shows the track lifted in 1965, and the third is the scene today. *Luke Kay (2), Mark Bartlett*

Not au revoir but goodbye to the Preston to Southport branch

Dereliction at Middleforth Junction, looking toward Whitehouse West. *Keith Hick*

Longton Bridge station in 1968, four years after closure. *Tony Graham*

In spring 1982 a Class 40 diesel stands at Southport Chapel Street, with steam trains just a memory. *Kenneth Grub, Roger Roberts collection*

A long-gone demolished bridge at Longton, with only the curious abutments left as a legacy of a branch line.

Stricklands Lane, Middleforth, Penwortham, in 2004.

The demolition of the WLR Ribble bridge seen from the lower Penwortham side of the river, in Preston, with two cranes working somewhat precariously over the river. Beyond can be glimpsed the first old Penwortham road bridge. *Luke Kay*

The remains of the WLR Ribble Bridge in September 2001. A pipe line is now carried by the stone piers. *Roger Roberts*

The viaduct on the approach to the Fishergate Hill station site being demolished. *Roger Roberts*

The WLR station at Fishergate Hill is seen from the south east corner. Having closed to goods traffic in 1965, it is awaiting demolition. *Fred Hartley*

The view from the ELR viaduct footbridge at Preston, with a close-up of a Stanier Class 5 heading for Lostock Hall. Beyond is the signal arm for Whitehouse West Junction, with the branch signal removed following closure. *Rob Greenwood*

The ELR viaduct looking north in September, 2001. *Roger Roberts*

The trackbed over Ivy Bridge, Preston. *Lancashire Libraries*

Not au revoir but goodbye to the Preston to Southport branch

The WLR bridge over Leyland Road, near the Bridge Inn in Penwortham, is demolished *(left and centre)*, and *(right)* the site today. *Ron Greenwood, Roger Roberts collection*

The melancholy site of Cop Lane station being demolished on 17 January 1965. *Alan Castle*

From rail to road: this is the view from Hill Road, Penwortham, looking towards Cop Lane, where the former Southport branch is now the Penwortham bypass. *Roger Roberts*

Left and above: The crossing gates at Nursery Lane, New Longton, before and after closure. *Alan Castle/Graeme Heaton*

Below left: The abutments of Longton Bridge mark the line's course through the village.

The ruined Crossens station in 1968. *Gordon Biddle*

Following closure, Crossens signal box has seen better days. *Tony Graham*

Dereliction at Hesketh Park station, August 1967. *Arnold Battson*

Not au revoir but goodbye to the Preston to Southport branch

An over-elaborate relic of Hesketh Drive Bridge, 31 March 2004. *Roger Roberts*

The demolition of Churchtown station in 1965. *Arnold Battson*

'Due to engineering work there will be no trains running today.' The demolition of Churchtown bridge. *David Regan*

St Luke's station had two widely separated island platform faces. Here, in 1968, demolition is taking place and no trace remains today. *Arnold Battson*

Right: A bridge at Botanic Gardens, Churchtown, Southport, in December 2006. *Roger Roberts*

Above: This view of Southport Chapel Street from Victoria Bridge on 31 April 2001 is looking towards St Luke's, but is bereft of marshalling yards, carriage sidings and two motive power depots. *Roger Roberts*

Right: Looking from Windsor Road towards St Luke's today, only the basic permanent way connecting Southport to Wigan and Manchester remains, Chapel Street lies behind the camera. *Roger Roberts*

12 • Memories: lament for a branch line

This final chapter features steam-hauled excursions and, on a note of unashamed nostalgia, some anecdotes and personal recollections of the Preston to Southport branch.

Steam hauled excursions

On Saturday 22 September 1962 the Railway Correspondence & Travel Society ran the 'Mid Lancs Rail Tour'. Its exciting itinerary was available for an inclusive fare of £1 6s, and included a visit to Fishergate Hill station for one last time. Appropriately, ex-LNWR Class 7F 0-8-0 No 49451 provided the motive power for the five-coach train of former LMS stock, comprising three corridor coaches, a half brake and a buffet car. At the same time it graphically placed on record a new form of railway mania being generated in the 1960s. Indeed, two of the three locomotives (including No 49451) to be used on various stages of the tour that day had previously been specially cleaned for the occasion by a small group of intending passengers!

The commemorative ticket for the RCTS 'Mid Lancs Rail Tour', which included a visit to the WLR Fishergate Hill station at Preston. *Alan Castle*

Above: 'Super D' 0-8-0 No 49451 pays a nostalgic visit to Longridge station on 22 September 1962 while hauling the RCTS tour along many closed branch lines. *Alan Castle*

Right: No 49451 is seen on arrival at the former Preston WLR station. *Peter Fitton*

On 23 May 1964 a most unusual visitor to the branch was BR 'Clan' 'Pacific' No 72007 *Clan Mackintosh*, working the RCTS 'Ribble/Lune' rail tour. The tour was interesting to say the least! Starting at Preston East Lancs Platform 13, with No 72007 up front, it travelled the Preston to Southport branch as far as Meols Cop, where it diverted at Butts Lane Junction to the Wigan line. From there the special was routed via the north Burscough Curve, Rufford, Bamber Bridge, Blackburn, Hellifield and Wennington, then along the now closed Lune Valley line via Caton, Lancaster Green Ayre and on to Heysham Harbour. From Heysham Ivatt No 46441 (now preserved) hauled the train to Morecambe Promenade station. Interestingly the 'Clan' then hauled the train tender-first from Morecambe Promenade via Hest Bank Junction, Lancaster Green Ayre and Lancaster Castle to the original station of the Lancaster & Preston Junction Railway at Lancaster Penny Street goods depot. The tour finished with *Clan Mackintosh* powering the train forward facing to Preston.

No 49451 waits to reverse out of Fishergate Hill station with the RCTS tour. *Peter Fitton*

Top right: At Penwortham Junction No 49451 is running wrong line towards Whitehouse West Junction, after reversing from Fishergate Hill *Peter Fitton*

On 23 May 1964 'Clan' No 72007 *Clan Mackintosh* stands at Preston's Platform 13 ready to work the RCTS 'Ribble/Lune' rail tour, which included the Southport branch but only as far as Roe Lane Junction, and Meols Cop, where the train diverted onto the Wigan line. *Alan Castle*

At Crossens station No 45642 *Boscowen* runs tender-first light engine from Preston to Southport to haul a stopping train from Southport to Preston on 5 September 1964. *Alan Castle*

No 45642 working 2P69, a stopping train, the 12.42pm, from Southport to Preston through Hoole station later that day. *Alan Castle*

In the 1960s there were several more steam-hauled excursions along the Preston to Southport branch, hauled by a variety of locomotives, including those seen in the accompanying photographs.

'Clan' 'Pacific' No 72007 *Clan Mackintosh* hauls the RCTS 'Ribble Lune' railtour on 23 May 1964, seen at the Balmoral Drive/Verulam Road footbridge. *Keith Hick*

'Britannia' 'Pacific' No 70010 *Owen Glendower* is assigned to excursion working at Southport on 17 May 1964.
Jim Peden, B. G. Barlow collection

Shared memories of the Preston to Southport branch

While there is now very little tangible evidence of the railway, memories are still sharp for the people who travelled the branch. Here were village communities that seemed to have been lost in the mists of time, when the railway was once their only contact with the outside world.

On 20 January 1965 Mrs A. Gwillam wrote a letter to the *Lancashire Evening Post*, remarkably recalling the old WLR Preston Fishergate Hill station in its glory days:

'Reading the article about the old West Lancashire Railway station at Preston brings back many happy memories. It was always such a clean station. One of the staff used to hang wire baskets of growing flowers, geraniums and marigolds.

In the 1890s the Southport fare was adults 1 shilling return (under 13 years sixpence). I am afraid I stayed under 13 for a long time. The trains were always well packed, especially at holiday times.

In those days the annual summer season holiday began on the third Saturday in August. There was no going away for a week – Saturday counted as a full day and we returned to work on the Thursday.

I wonder if anyone still living went on the trip to Hull (fare 3s 6d return), which my friend and I took one Whitsuntide (departing 6.00am and returning to Preston at 2.00am).

The fare to Blackpool by the old L&Y Railway was 1s 6d return.'

*

Tom Alty of Bartle, one-time resident of Hesketh Bank, recalls cattle being offloaded at Hesketh Bank station from Ireland. He has vivid memories of the Banks women dressed in dark skirts and starched pinafores taking Southport-caught shrimps to Preston market in large wicker baskets.

*

An interesting story is recounted by a Mr Ashcroft who as a boy was taken on a journey by his Uncle Dick to a place he pronounced in the vernacular as "Thunder Den". These words caused the boy's imagination to wander among monsters with green claws breathing fire. It was only on the train's arrival that the boy realised his uncle's pronunciation of their destination was in fact the rural Lancashire dialect for Hundred End (Ashcroft, 1976: 60).

*

Mr Burton of Penwortham related details of a career on the railway, retiring as a signalman at Preston No 5 box. He started as a Junior Porter at

Memories: lament for a branch line

New Longton & Hutton station in 1958. At that time trains started from Preston at about 6.00am and the last train returned from Southport at about 11.00pm. As a Junior Porter on late turn, Mr Burton would be left on his own to collect tickets from disembarking passengers on the last train, before quickly locking up the station buildings and boarding the train for home. It was a frequent occurrence, and a source of amusement for the driver, aided and abetted by the fireman, to start the train for Preston before young Mr Burton had finished his tasks, causing him to run at full speed to catch the last train of the day.

*

Leslie Harrison of Longton recalls an amusing and interesting story that occurred just before the line closed.

When the line was first built it was a requirement of the Act of Parliament that the bridge over the River Douglas, near Hesketh Bank, must be constructed to allow the passage of high-masted vessels along the river. Therefore to comply with the legislature a swing bridge was constructed.

In the early 1960s the owner of a yacht wanted to bring his vessel to moorings upstream of the railway bridge, having sailed up the River Douglas from the River Ribble. In the knowledge that the mast was too tall to go under the bridge, he duly contacted British Railways to ask them to swing the bridge open to facilitate navigation upriver. However, he was informed that his request had to be denied as the bridge structure had been permanently welded in the closed position, due to maintenance costs and a reduction of river traffic.

The yachtsman pointed out that the Parliamentary Act requiring the bridge to open had never been repealed. The issue was resolved by British Railways, which admitted its error and funded the owner of the yacht to moor his vessel downstream of the bridge at the Douglas Boatyard.

Aye aye, skipper!

*

The Preston to Southport line, together with the Altcar branch, embodied the character of rural railways in bygone Lancashire. Long before the widespread use of the automobile, both lines were inextricably linked to a pattern of rural life, pastoral countryside that was a haven for local wildlife, and rural communities that relied on their local branch line. The white plumes of smoke that drifted over the fields accompanied by the shrill whistle and exhaust blasts of hard-working locomotives contrasted with the charismatic calls of curlews, lapwings and pink-footed geese flying in 'v' formation from the Ribble marshes, perhaps outshone by skylarks ascending with their sustained melody of song. Today such quintessential elements of avian excellence are in freefall decline, and a similar analogy might be applied to the network of local railways that were once pivotal to the rural landscape of England – rural branch lines and a way of community life that now seems long gone. Gone, perhaps, but not entirely forgotten!

An ignominious end to a branch line: a view through the arch of a bridge towards the ruination of Cop Lane station. *Author*

Above: No 61050 at Twigg Molls with a Hull-Southport Flower Show excursion in August 1961.

Right: Metrovick Co-Bo No D5709 with a Barrow-Southport excursion in the summer of 1962.

The railway photographs of Keith Hick FISTC MSAI AIAM

Growing up in the 1950s and early 1960s, with a railway line alongside the garden of my parents' house in Churchtown, Southport, guaranteed a lifelong love of trains, railways and model railways. The 180-degree panorama of the railway I enjoyed from my bedroom window lit the touch paper of my love of trains and the world of railways. The sight and sound of trains, both electric and steam, rumbling by instilled a sense of routine and stability in a young mind. The trains always got through – winter, summer, ice and snow, fog, storms, occasional excessive heat – nothing seemed to stop them. Late-night pigeon specials, excursion trains from afar and the early morning electric de-icing units lighting up the gloom with their lightning-like flashes clearing the rails; each and every one left indelible memories to last a lifetime. 'Permanent way' is a well-understood term in railway circles and the excellent state of the manicured track running past our house, electrified as far as Crossens, embodied the sense of pride of the track gangs as they went about their everyday maintenance tasks. How quickly we came to realise there is no such thing as 'permanence' with the over-hasty ripping up of the track during March 1965, within six months of closure in September 1964.

The old adage of 'the sound of silence was deafening' aptly summed up the loss of the railway. I didn't realise at the time, but the feelings were one of bereavement. Overnight, all sounds ceased, as did the much-missed train service to Preston, one of the most grievous losses to Southport's economy.

No 44756 is at the head of the 8.00am Southport-Accrington train in February 1964, seen from the trackside.

Tom Lally's atmospheric rendition of Churchtown station in the 1930s The Southport-Preston line was known alternatively as the 'Shrimper's Line' and 'Lettuce Line' thanks to the close proximity of the local fisherfolk and market gardeners dispatching their catch and produce far and wide from stations along the line. *Courtesy of Keith Hick*

Right: 'Clan' Class 'Pacific' No 72007 *Clan Mackintosh* passes Roe Lane Junction on 23 May 1964 with the RCTS excursion

Memories: lament for a branch line

No 44686 is captured from the photographer's bedroom window on a Southport-Preston service in the summer of 1964.

No 44756 is at the head of the 8.00am Southport-Accrington train in February 1964, also seen from the photographer's bedroom window.

Memories: lament for a branch line

Above: Rebuilt 'Patriot' No 45525 stands at Meols Cop station with the 6.00pm Manchester (Victoria)-Southport business express in the summer of 1964.

Above right: No 78041 is captured between Churchtown and Hesketh Park with a Preston-Southport service, summer 1964.

Right: No 44686 passes Roe Lane Junction on 12 June 1964.

Above left: No 44745 at Hesketh Park in June 1964.

Above: 'Jubilee' No 45596 *Bahamas* runs between Hesketh Park and Churchtown with the 8.05am Southport-Preston train in June 1964.

Left: Super power for the 2.14pm Preston-Southport train on 23 May 1964 as Caprotti Class 5 4-6-0 No 44686 is about to pass beneath the vantage point of Twigg Molls footbridge. The author's bedroom window can be seen to the right of the locomotive's chimney. A set of catch points can also be seen alongside the permanent way hut, installed to derail any runaway rolling stock into the adjacent field before it could reach Hesketh Park station.

No 44756 heads towards Hesketh Park, again seen from Twigg Molls footbridge on the same day.

Lament for a Branch Line

Above: A drawing of the Bibby Road subway by Cecil M. Barton.

Left: A DMU on a returning excursion from Ayr on 30 August 1964.

Below: A plan of Churchtown station in 1890, drawn by Keith Hick.

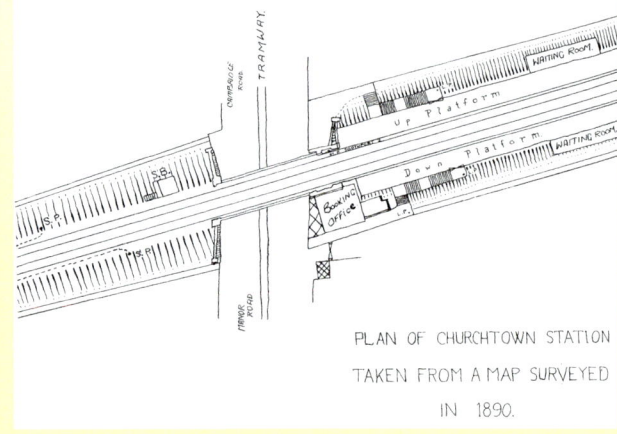

Memories: lament for a branch line

The last ticket issued from Churchtown station on 6 September 1964.

Stanier Class 5 4-6-0 No 44767 (now preserved and named *George Stephenson*) fitted with Stephenson link valve gear, passes with an early morning Southport-Preston service during 1964. No 44767 joined several Caprotti valve gear Class 5 4-6-0s at Southport shed during the early 1960s, working daily trains to Manchester, Bolton and Preston.

Left: Stanier Class 5 4-6-0 No 44940 builds up a good turn of speed with a returning excursion to Accrington on 23 May 1964.

Above: Ex-LMS EMU No M29865M heads towards Churchtown station with a Southport (Chapel Street)-Crossens service on 8 August 1964. These long-serving units, introduced in 1939 by the LMS to replace the original Lancashire & Yorkshire Railway EMUs of 1904, remained in service until 1980. A two-car unit comprising power car and driving trailer was retained by the National Railway Museum and returned to working order.

Class 5 4-6-0 No 45216 ambles downgrade from Churchtown with the 5.25pm Blackburn-Southport service on 27 May 1964. A daily early morning Monday-Friday businessmen's service, leaving Southport (Chapel Street) at 8.00am and returning at 5.25pm, was complemented by a Saturday's only (SO) Colne-Southport and return service during the summer timetable.

Hesketh Park yard seen from the signal box in February 1965.

Above left: Fairburn tank No 42078 at the site of Churchtown station with a track-lifting train in March 1965.

Above: One last look towards Churchtown station on 5 September 1964, two days before closure.

Left: Track-lifting is in progress alongside the photographer's parents' house in Churchtown, March 1965.

Above: Crossens goods yard is seen after the lifting of the track, looking towards Preston in March 1965.

Right: A view of the trackless Crossens station in March 1965.

Below: Track-lifting in Churchtown, also in March 1965.

Right: Another view of the track being lifted at the site of Churchtown station, March 1965.

Below left: Track-lifting at Twigg Molls footbridge, between Churchtown and Hesketh Park, in March 1965.

Above: Track-lifting operations are seen from the footbridge in the same month.

Left: The track-lifting foreman, Walter (surname unknown), poses with the engine driver near Hesketh Park in April 1965.

Opposite page: Station totem signs: Hesketh Park, Banks, St Lukes, Meols Cop and Churchtown.

Appendix One - Serious railway accident at Whitehouse Triangle on 13 May 1950: extract fom the official report

At 10.25pm on 13 May 1950 a serious railway accident at Whitehouse West Junction, near the overbridge carrying the WCML, involved a passenger train and a stationary light steam engine. There were 80 passengers on the train, of whom eight were seriously injured, 15 others were treated in hospital but not detained, and 40 others sustained minor injuries and suffered shock.

The 10.20pm passenger train from Preston to Southport, comprising four carriages behind a 2-6-2T travelling bunker-first under clear signals at about 20mph, collided with a stationary Class 8F 2-8-0 facing towards Southport. The passenger locomotive was derailed and badly damaged; none of the coaches were derailed. The light engine suffered little damage and was not derailed.

The driver of the light engine said he had been instructed to turn his engine round the Whitehouse triangle. After passing Whitehouse South Junction he saw the West Junction signal 'off' and ran 10 yards beyond the trailing points at the Southport end and waited for the crossover to be reversed. The driver of the passenger train said he had a clear run with all the signals 'off', but as he passed Whitehouse West Junction box his fireman shouted that there was an engine in front. He applied his brakes but the collision occurred.

The Inspector's report on behalf of the Ministry of Transport held the signalman as being primarily responsible. He had accepted the passenger train without making any proper attempt to satisfy himself that the line was clear. The driver of the light engine should share some of the responsibility in that he and his fireman had been talking and drinking tea, and neither of them realised how long they had been waiting. There was also a contravention of Rule 55 – it was the driver's responsibility to have sent his fireman to the box immediately after he had been detained on the running line at the crossover, and he was not paying attention to his duties.

Appendix Two - The ex-L&YR Aspinall Class 2P 'Radial' 2-4-2Ts at Southport

The 2P 'Radial' 2-4-2T locomotives, the work of Sir John Audley Frederick Aspinall, were a Victorian anachronism that survived into the era of British Railways at Southport.

Aspinall was a fully trained locomotive engineer, President of the Institution of Civil Engineers and a Director of the L&YR. He introduced the 'Radial' tanks in 1889 for working suburban passenger services, and in their prime they hauled express trains to Fleetwood and Blackpool, and Southport to Manchester. Several of the class were allocated to Southport and finished their days there in the early 1960s. One such example was No 50850, seen in the accompanying photographs.

No 50850 leaves Southport with a passenger train in May 1960. Note the excursion platforms on the right.
J. H. Turner

Appendix Two - The ex-L&YR Aspinall Class 2P 'Radial' 2-4-2Ts at Southport

No 50850 is working as station pilot at Southport on 24 May 1960. *Arnold Battson*

A few weeks later No 50850 is seen again at Southport, on 3 June 1960. *Jim Peden*

No 50850 is again on station pilot duties on home ground on 6 July 1961. *Jim Peden*

A clean No 50850 was photographed alongside the cattle pens at Southport on 28 September 1961. *Roger Roberts collection*

Another of the ex-L&YR Aspinall 2-4-2Ts, LMS No 10743, is seen at Southport on 18 August 1939. *Roger Carpenter collection*

2-4-2T No 50712 hauls the 5.07pm Southport to Preston passenger train at Hesketh Park on 3 August 1956. *Ribble Steam Railway*

Bibliography

Primary sources held at Southport Town Hall and Library in Box 625/11

West Lancashire Railway: Acquisition of railway, plans and additional lands
Liverpool, Southport & Preston Junction Railway: Plans and references insofar as relates to North Meols
Southport and Cheshire Lines Extension Railway: as above

Entries in newspapers - See index for entries in the *Southport Visiter* and *Southport Guardian*

The following maps show the relevant railway routes:
Maps No 17B (1893), 22 (c1900), 38 (1939 directory)

Ordnance Survey 25-inch maps (1892-1894)

See indexes to prints, photographs and circulars, and Ward Lock Guide to Southport, 1887

Primary sources held at the Lancashire Record Office, Preston

DDX 87/67 Railway Timetable
DDX 1576 Maps of Preston (Butler Street) station
DDX 1042/4 Airey's map of Lancashire (1894)
DDX 1042/9-11 Miscellaneous photographs
DDPR 144/12 Map of West Lancashire Railway
DDX 693/6 WLR letters – one from Lord Derby dated 19.11.1845
DDX 490/1-4 L&YR report and accounts 1894-96
DDX 712 Maps and plans
DDH 77/79 Agreement of 1894 between WLR and Sir Thomas George Fermor-Hesketh of Rufford Hall with plan of Hundred End station
DDH 1145-1152 Petition of WLR bid and hand-written letters (1894)
CBP 60/8 WLR 1869/1870 Bill and documents
CBP 60/10 WLR Act, 1871
CBP 60/10 Letters between lawyers and Preston Borough Council re dimension of Ribble railway bridge
Various documents concerning the WLR Bill, 1871

Bibliography

Secondary sources - books

Ashcroft, J. *Steam Up in Lancashire: On the Track of Altcar Bob* (Whitethorn Press, 1976)

Ashcroft, T. H. *Steam Up in Lancashire: Thunder Den* (Whitethorn Press, 1976)

Aughton, P. *North Meols and Southport* (Carnegie Publishing, 1988)

Biddle, G. *Scenes From the Past 6: The Railways Around Preston, An Historical Review* (Foxline)

British Railways Board London Midland Region. Memorandum to the Chairman and Members of the North Western Area Transport Users Consultative Committee, August 1963

Cook, R. A. *Lancashire & Yorkshire Railway Historical Maps* (Railway & Canal History Society, 1976)

Cotterall, J. *North Meols to South Ribble* (Richardson, 1985) *The West Lancashire Railway* (Oakwood, 1982)

Earnshaw, A. *The Lancashire & Yorkshire Railway Then and Now* (Ian Allan, 1992)

Gammell, C. J. *LMS Branch Lines* (Haynes, 1991)

Greville, M. D. *Chronology of the Railways of Lancashire* (Railway & Canal Historical Society, 1973)

West Lancashire Mysteries (Railway & Canal Historical Society, 1960)

Griffin, S. A. 'Sir Edward Watkin' (*Backtrack* magazine, Volume 12, No 12, pp659-661, December 1998

Griffiths, R. P. *The Cheshire Lines Railway* (Oakwood Press, 1958)

Hartley-Bracewell, W. 'Sunny Southport: The Cheshire Lines' (*The Railway Magazine*, Volume 2, January-June 1898

Hindle, D. J. *All Stations to Longridge* (Amberley Publishing, 2010)

Preston Planes, Trains, Tramcars and Ships (Amberley Publishing, 2015)

Enjoying the Cumbrian Coast Railway (Silver Link Publishing, 2019)

By Rail to the Music Halls (Silver Link Publishing and Mortons Media Group, 2020)

Holt, G. O. *A Regional History of the Railways of Great Britain: Volume 10 The North West* (David & Charles, 1978)

Hunt, D. *A History of Preston* (Carnegie Publishing, 1992)

Marshall J. *Forgotten Railways: North West England* (David & Charles, 1981)

The Lancashire & Yorkshire Railway, Volume 1 (David & Charles, 1969); *Volume 3* (David & Charles, 1972)

Mason, E. *The Lancashire & Yorkshire Railway in the Twentieth Century* (Ian Allan, 1954)

Morgan, N. *Deadly Dwellings: Housing and Public Health in a Lancashire Cotton Town: Preston from 1840 to 1914* (Mullion Books, 1993)

Simmons, J. and Biddle, G. *The Oxford Companion to British Railway History* (Oxford University Press, 1997)

The Locomotive Magazine and Railway Carriage and Wagon Review, Volume 14, Nos 309-311, May-June 1918)

Wareing, C. *Gradely Bonksers: A History of Banks* (Author, published locally, date unknown)

Whittingham, T. E. *More About Hesketh and Becconsall* (Author, published locally, 1985)

Working Timetable of Passenger Trains Between Preston, Southport and Liverpool Exchange and Branches, 15 June-6 September 1964 (British Railways London Midland Region)

Baxter (1982) *British Locomotive Catalogue 1825-1923 Volume 3B*

Roberts (2000) The West Lancashire Railway

Acknowledgements

I am extremely grateful to Sir Peter Hendy CBE, Chairman of Network Rail, for doing me the honour of writing such a constructive foreword. I acknowledge and remember with affection my friend the late Roger Ronald Roberts, to whom the book is dedicated. Roger inspired my research and knowledge and bequeathed to me his entire photographic portfolio of the Preston to Southport line, to share with all railway historians and enthusiasts. I am obliged to my good friend, David Eaves for his technical help and excellent maps and diagrams.

Research has encompassed a wide range of primary sources. In addition to the National Railway Museum library, I acknowledge the help of librarians at Southport and Preston, Lancashire Archives and the Public Record Office at Kew.

I am indebted to all photographers for their considerable photographic skills including Stan Withers, Peter Fitton, Bob Gregson, Richard Casserley, Gordon Biddle, Keith Hick, Mark Bartlett, John Williams, Arnold Battson, David Hampson, the late Jim Peden and Alan Castle. All the private collections of photographs are subject to copyright, and permission has been granted to reproduce them with an appropriate acknowledgement. Thanks also to journalists of long ago who wrote in local newspapers about the social impact of railways on local communities. I thank all contributors, while pointing out that I have made every effort to trace copyright owners of illustrative and textual material, though this has sometimes proved very difficult. I therefore apologise for any possible omissions.

Finally I would like to thank my publisher Steve O'Hara at Morton's publishing and Peter Townsend at Slip Coach Publishing for his dedication in making this new work possible.

Index of locations

Altcar & Hillhouse 30, 31, 47, 49, 50, 54-56, 57, 75
Ash Street *see* St Luke's

Banks 5, 6, 7, 14, 17, 75, 76, 88, 109-11, 128, 138
Barton *see* Downholland
Boatyard Crossing Halt (Tarleton) 60, 61
Burscough Bridge 27, 32, 33, 142
Butts Lane Halt, Southport 50

Churchtown 8, 11, 39, 69, 70, 75, 82, 112-13, 137, 143, 149, 158, 160, 164-67, 168, 169, 170
Crossens 19, 39, 61, 69, 78, 79, 81, 88, 90, 93, 111, 133, 137, 138, 148, 153, 169

Douglas, River, swing bridge over at Hesketh Bank 5, 16, 35, 58-59, 61, 62, 73, 106, 135, 155; station 35, 58, 60
Downholland 47, 50, 52, 53, 54, 57

Halsall 47, 48, 52-53, 56
Hawkshead Street Junction 27, 78-79, 80, 81, 94
Heathey Lane Halt 50
Hesketh Bank 6, 16, 27, 32, 34, 35, 58, 60, 62, 64, 67, 69, 74, 76, 88, 92, 106-08, 135, 139, 142, 154
Hesketh Park 16, 32, 34, 38, 67, 69, 75, 76, 83, 88, 89, 90, 114-15, 125, 136, 137, 143, 148, 149, 162, 168, 170
Hillhouse Junction 27, 47, 54
Hoghton 21
Hoole 14, 35, 36, 88, 90, 93, 105-06, 139, 153
Howick/Hutton & Howick *see* New Longton & Hutton
Hundred End 6, 8, 76, 77, 88, 108-09, 132-33, 138, 154

Kew Gardens 47, 51

Lindle Lane crossing 90, 93, 101
Long Lane 18
Longton (Bridge) 16, 35, 36, 72, 75, 76, 88, 104-05, 124, 139, 143, 145, 148

Meols Cop and triangle 27, 47, 78, 80-81, 161; Electric Maintenance Depot 81, 82, 136
Middleforth Junction 33, 46, 145

New Cut Lane Halt 50
New Longton & Hutton 1, 6, 36, 37, 88, 92, 102-04, 125, 127, 128, 140, 148

Penwortham, and triangle 5, 33, 34, 38, 46, 75, 98, 99, 142, 147, 152, 155
Penwortham Cop Lane 5, 9, 36, 38, 99-101, 135, 140, 141, 147, 155
Pleasington 21
Plex Moss Lane Halt 50
Poole Hey Junction 47
Preston 9, 10, 11, 12-13, 20-22, 75, 83, 87, 89, 91, 92, 93, 95-98, 134, 135, 136, 141, 142, 153; Butler Street 21, 24, 25, 26; ELR viaduct 7, 22-23, 97, 98, 142, 145-46; Fishergate Hill (WLR) 16, 20, 28, 38, 39-41, 46, 67, 70, 73, 88, 98, 135, 142, 146, 151-52; Ivy Bridge 24, 25, 146; Junction 68-69; signal boxes 25, 26

Ribble Junction 46
Roe Lane Junction 27, 47, 78, 79, 131, 136, 159, 161

St Luke's 17, 75, 76, 77, 86, 90, 115-16, 126, 127, 149

Shirdley Hill 47, 49, 52, 56
Southport 12-16, 24, 27, 73, 77, 122, 124, 129; Central 27, 28, 29, 39, 42, 70, 77, 78; Chapel Street 8, 28, 31, 50, 52, 69, 77, 78, 82, 83, 84, 87, 91, 94, 116-20, 121, 122- 24, 125, 126, 131, 134, 136, 140, 141, 145, 150, 154, 172-74; Kensington Road 41, 42, 77, 78, 88; Lakeside Miniature Railway 129; loco shed 67-68, 85, 86, 87, 89, 116-18; Lord Street 29-30, 31; Windsor Road 35, 38, 39, 63, 67, 69, 150

Square House Lane 18-19

Tarleton branch 58ff, 75
Todd Lane Junction 22
Twigg Molls 156, 163, 170

Whitehouse Triangle (North, South and West Junctions) 21, 22, 33, 42-46, 75, 91, 136, 142, 143, 144, 156